For the Survivors

Cover design: Clockwork Cuckoo,
background photo Old Merthyr Tydfil.
Photographs from contributors' own collections
are reproduced with permission. Archive photos of the
disaster are reproduced with permission by Old Merthyr
Tydfil and Media Wales.
Photograph of Jeff Edwards by IC Rapoport reproduced with
permission.
Present day portraits by Emily Sivyer.
The Price of Coal by permission of Esther Mayo.

This book is published by
Grosvenor House Publishing Ltd
28-30 High Street, Guildford, Surrey, GU1 3EL.
www.grosvenorhousepublishing.co.uk

A CIP record for this book
is available from the British Library

ISBN 978-1-78623-034-8

THE PRICE OF COAL

For 200 years my people were miners
And dug in the mountains and valleys of Wales.
I grew to my manhood knowing their stories
And the price of the coal was the soul of these tales.

I knew of the fire and the fall and the famine
I knew of the lockout and strike and the dole.
I knew of the anger sharpened by hunger
I knew of the price that was paid for the coal.

But brothers, believe me, I never saw equal
When Aberfan drowned in the slag and the slime.
For never before was the price paid in children
And a whole generation was killed in that crime.

And people are kind and there's money in plenty
But giving is easy and losing is dear.
And all of the kindness can't comfort the aching.
Oh, the price of the coal, it was priceless that year.

Charles Mayo 1966

CONTENTS

FOREWORD

By Jeff Edwards MBE

On 21st October 1966 a small mining village 20 miles north of Cardiff and four miles south of Merthyr Tydfil became the centre of attention for the world's media. After a while the media moved on, but Aberfan would remain in the hearts and minds of the nation forever.

Early on that morning waste coal tip material from the No. 7 tip situated high above the village would come rolling down the mountainside, hitting the arterial water main from the Brecon Beacons reservoirs to Cardiff and forming a black sludge that would engulf everything in its path, including the Pantglas Junior School, wiping out a generation of young people who were looking forward to the autumn half term.

In this man-made disaster 116 children and 28 adults would perish, dying of physical injuries and asphyxiation after being buried in the school and many surrounding buildings that were destroyed in the process. The children who survived would live with a burden of guilt. Why had they lived while their friends died? Bereaved parents would have to deal with the emotional loss of one or more children. Rescuers would have to come to terms with the carnage they faced in the rescue and the recovery operations that followed. And a whole community would mourn the loss of a generation whose young lives were brought to such a tragic end.

As an eight year-old child I was buried in the school. I was the last to be brought out of the school alive – and the last survivor to be rescued. My physical injuries would heal but it was the psychological injuries that would have the greatest effect on me and will be with me for the rest of my life. I left the village in 1976 to pursue a university education and career in London, but was drawn back to the community following the closure of the local colliery, Merthyr Vale, in 1989. I became actively involved as a Councillor, Mayor and Leader of the Council in the regeneration of the community, following the decimation of the South Wales coalfield and the social and economic deprivation it caused.

This year, 2016, marks the 50th anniversary of the disaster and for many in the community that day is as raw now as it was 50 years ago. Whilst the years and decades have gone by, the memory of Aberfan has not faded but remains in the psychology of the nation, and people from all over the world still visit to pay their respects. Whilst the loss affected everyone in the community and the journey to recovery has been tortuous and hard, the message from Aberfan is that there is light at the end of a very dark tunnel and that a community can regenerate itself into a happy vibrant place to live, whilst still remembering the tragedy of the past.

This book records the personal testimony of individuals who have contributed their memories of their involvement in the disaster, many of whom have not told their stories publicly before. It represents a unique collective testimony of survivors, bereaved parents and rescuers, that tells of their individual experiences on that awful day and afterwards.

I commend it to you as a unique collection of personal memories that are a fitting tribute by those who were directly involved in a tragedy I hope the world will never forget.

AUTHORS' NOTE &
ACKNOWLEDGEMENTS

This book is based on transcripts of interviews conducted by Steve Humphries of Testimony Films with 27 people directly involved in the Aberfan disaster for the television documentary *Surviving Aberfan,* broadcast by the BBC in October 2016. Interviews were transcribed and edited for length, by topic, and to reduce unnecessary repetition, otherwise we believe they faithfully reproduce what people said and how they said it.

Steve would like to thank Adrian Davies, BBC Wales Head of English Language Programmes and Services, Christina Macaulay, BBC Wales Executive Producer, Clare Paterson, BBC Documentaries and Factual Commissioning Editor, and Cassian Harrison, Editor BBC4, for their initial support in making this project happen and for their advice throughout.

At Testimony Films assistant producer Emily Sivyer worked tirelessly for nine months on the project and with great sensitivity helped form a bond of trust with the people of Aberfan which made filming of the interviews possible. Film editor and producer Andy Attenburrow played an invaluable role in shaping the programme from beginning to end. Development producer Dave Long helped get the project off the ground. Archivist Lucy McFadzean did valuable work transcribing some of the interviews. And assistant producers Pete Vance and Lizi Cosslett provided professional back-up throughout. We would also like to thank cameramen Stephen J Brand, Rhys Edwards, Stephen Hart and Andrew Lewis and for their sensitive filming of the interviews.

For background detail on the rescue effort, the Tribunal of Inquiry and other aspects of the disaster and its aftermath we have leant heavily on two excellent but very different books: *Aberfan: Government and Disasters* by Iain McLean and Martin Johnes (Welsh Academic Press 2000) and *Aberfan: the story of a disaster* by Tony Austin (Hutchinson 1967). Gaynor Madgwick's memoir, *Aberfan: A Story of Survival, Love and Community in One of Britain's Worst Disasters* (Y Lolfa 2016) was also very useful in providing another survivor's perspective.

Thank you to Sally Humphries and Averina Humphries (no relation) for their help. However our biggest debt of gratitude is to the people of Aberfan. Thanks are due to the Aberfan Wives group, the Ynysowen Male Voice Choir, Aberfan Community Library and Gareth Jones for access to his valuable archive. Most of all we wish to thank the people who agreed to be interviewed and to the many family members who assisted us. They all gave up so much of their time to contribute to the documentary and this book. We are only too well aware how difficult appearing on camera was for many of them, especially those who had chosen not to speak publicly before. We thank them all for their courage and their patience.

They are, in alphabetical order, **Professor Sir Mansel Aylward, Marilyn Brown, Dorothy Burns, Gloria Davies, Malcolm Davies, Mary Davies, Sheila Davies, Jeff Edwards MBE, Tessie Edwards, Bob Griffiths, Len Haggett, Roy Hamer, Calvin Hodkinson, David Hopkins, Joyce Hughes, Gareth Jones, Allan Lewis, Denise Morgan MBE, Mary Morse, Gerald Tarr, Alan Thomas, Bernard Thomas, Dave Thomas, Karen Thomas, Phil Thomas, June Vaughan** and **Hettie Williams** (née Taylor).

Sue Elliott
Steve Humphries
Bevan Jones   Summer 2016

INTRODUCTION

2016 marks the 50th anniversary of the Aberfan disaster. The people of this Welsh mining village, where life for more than a century revolved around the Merthyr Vale colliery, have rarely spoken at length about what happened to them on 21st October 1966, and for good reason. On that morning, at the start of the school day, a massive tip slide careered down the mountainside, engulfing the village primary school and surrounding houses in thousands of tons of rubble and coal waste, killing 116 children and 28 adults.

Aberfan ranks high among the worst peacetime UK disasters of the 20th century: the loss of so many children in what should have been their safe haven shocked Wales, Britain and the world. The impact was immediate, the public response overwhelming in messages of condolence and gifts in cash and kind.

For those of us old enough to remember the tragedy the bare, terrible facts and those stark black and white television and newspaper images of that day and its immediate aftermath are easily recalled, though the detail may have grown hazy over the decades and the unfolding story of official mismanagement and worse that followed was always less well known. But for the people of Aberfan who were there and those rescuers first on the scene, images of what they saw and what they experienced that day cannot so easily be erased by time. Nor can the after-effects of trauma be so easily repaired.

Inevitably, talking about the disaster brings back acutely painful memories and the return of unwelcome physical and psychological symptoms. Because of this many have found sharing their experience just too difficult. As one survivor told us, talking *'releases from your subconscious those things that many people have hidden away, been unable to speak about, and that's not because they don't want to speak about them. It's because they can't.'*

This was a common experience for many of the people we interviewed. One described it like this: *'No, I couldn't speak about it. I just couldn't. I'd start talking and I'd be very emotional about it. It's like having a brand new film in the camera, and you've taken a photograph and that photograph never goes away. It's always there.'*

But even those who find it most difficult to speak publicly understand that the story of Aberfan and what happened afterwards is too important to be allowed to lapse in public memory. Though the official record appeared in the Tribunal of Inquiry, subsequent academic studies provided valuable analysis, and hundreds of newspaper, magazine and television reports told the immediate human story, the individual testimonies of survivors, rescuers, bereaved parents and all those close to them are still largely unheard.

After 50 years some of those people are no longer here to tell their stories. Many of the bereaved parents are now in their 80s and 90s. A significant number are now buried with their children in Bryntaf cemetery. Even the youngest of those who were children at the time are now approaching their 60s. So, at this significant anniversary, it is probably the last opportunity we have to capture this experience from the widest number of surviving witnesses.

This is what we've tried to do in this book and in the BBC television documentary *Surviving Aberfan*. We promised the people we interviewed that their stories would form part of a permanent oral history archive. To augment this book and to leave as complete a record as possible, arrangements are being made for transcripts of their interviews and the filmed interviews themselves to be lodged in public archives for future access and research.

The fact that surviving witnesses form a slowly vanishing community has made it more important to people in Aberfan that their story be told – and remembered – in their own words. As the years have passed, many have had time to reflect on what happened and reconcile old hurts with the moderating effects of subsequent experience. Feelings and experiences they were once unable to put into words and share with others can now start to be articulated.

Motivations for this vary. Many believe it is vital that the full story of what happened to their community should never be forgotten, so they are willing to talk – perhaps for the first time – on the record. Some who survived the ordeal when others had not and who perhaps have suffered what subsequently became recognised as 'survivor's guilt' have been reticent for decades out of respect for the dead and the bereaved, but believe that now is finally the time to speak out. One adult survivor told us: *'I've waited 50 years to give these interviews... After 50 years I will talk about it now. And the reason for that is, if the mothers and fathers [are] reading what I went through, they might have thought their kids went through it. So that's why I wouldn't give interviews until now'.*

Others wanted placed on record the largely unsung role of the emergency services and the men who risked their lives in rescue operations in the most challenging conditions and who lived thereafter haunted by regret that they couldn't have brought out more alive. At the time these men – though deeply affected by the experience – rationalised it as 'just a part of the job', chose not to discuss it and tried to forget. One told us: *'I didn't want to fetch it back in my memory... it was never coming out in the open. Not only for myself, I didn't want to impose them pictures on other people of what we'd seen and dealt with in Aberfan that day'.*

But Aberfan is too exceptional and too important to be forgotten. A former fireman told us: *'If we don't say what happened that day, then it will never be known. Many of the officers who were there that day have now gone, passed on. I felt that [their actions] should be recorded somewhere along the way. Maybe as a lesson for others, I don't know, but that was my feelings'.*

Yet others want to demonstrate to the world that Aberfan, though the scene of great tragedy, has rebuilt itself and its community and is stronger now than ever. That the physical regeneration of the valleys, with the scars left by mining now all but healed and Nature reclaimed, has been matched by community regeneration. Though that great engine of South Wales' industrial clout and of Britain's prosperity, coal mining, has gone, 'w*e still have an important role in the life of the nation... as a great place to live, work and to play* '.

I believe that personal oral histories support and enhance the official record, fill in the human gaps, give perspective and convey complex emotions. That's why I set up Testimony Films 25 years ago to help people tell important stories that otherwise might not be heard. For Aberfan, just as important as the horrific detail of the day and its immediate aftermath is what happened much later: how lives have been lived through difficult times, but also how so many positives have come out of the tragedy. It is striking how often the burden of painful memories is lifted in these testimonies by talk of laughter, inspiring friendship and family ties, hope for the future.

For everyone who decided to talk to us on camera and for this book, it was something of an ordeal and we don't underestimate the personal cost of having to recall such intimate and painful experiences, perhaps from long-suppressed memory. It was a uniquely emotional experience for them, and for us. As a programme-maker who has conducted around 1500 interviews – including with 9/11 survivors and rescuers – for over 200 historical documentaries, I found these some of the most affecting I have ever done.

So we all owe them a debt of gratitude for their willingness to endure this exposure for the public record. It took much soul-searching before they came forward and we would like to pay tribute to them, and to those who were able to encourage them by making the first tentative moves. Aberfan is still a close community, like all of Wales welcoming to visitors but slow to share its most painful secrets with strangers, preferring to take comfort and support from among its own. We must respect that but we should also discharge our duty – and their wish – to tell these very personal histories of the Aberfan disaster of 1966.

Steve Humphries

1

LIFE BEFORE

Aberfan in the 1960s was typical of dozens of villages scattered along the valleys of the South Wales coalfield. 'Villages' is misleading; they were more like small self-contained towns. They were there because the river valleys running down from the southern edge of the Brecon Beacons towards Cardiff and the coast still contained huge quantities of high-quality coal: coal that fed ironworks, powered ships and factories, and heated homes across Britain. Like so many villages in the valleys, coal was Aberfan's life-blood, as Jeff Edwards recalls from his childhood.

> The village of Aberfan was a mining community... supplying coal to the power station in Barry and in people's houses because in the 1960s they all burned coal at home.

Merthyr Vale colliery was the pumping heart of the community and it determined everything else that went on in the village.

> The colliery was on the floor of the valley and was the hive of activity, providing employment and most families were associated with coal mining. Basically they fell out of bed into work, they didn't have far to go. The village itself was a thriving community. There were plenty of shops, a newsagent, butchers, bakers, ironmonger, chemists, men's and ladies' clothes shops. It was a

bustling community and you didn't have to go out of the village to get any of the essentials of life. There was a cinema and a Miners' Hall where local people went to enjoy themselves, as well as the pubs.

During the course of the 1960s the number of collieries was gradually shrinking as successive governments' pit closure policies proceeded by stealth. Falling demand and rising production costs meant that in Britain's biggest nationalised industry there were too many pits and too many miners. Former Union man Lord Alfred Robens had been entrusted to halve the number of pits with the minimum of industrial unrest. But those still in production, like Merthyr Vale, continued to bring jobs and modest prosperity to their communities. The valleys had recovered from the Depression of the 1930s and come through the Second World War largely unscathed by bombing, unlike their less fortunate city neighbours. The arrival of the Hoover factory in Merthyr in 1948 offered another source of secure employment. So Aberfan lived a settled way of life that had, by the time of the disaster, been stable for several generations.

Alongside the well-established routines and certainties of life in the valleys, hard work was a given. Like many of his contemporaries Gerald Tarr went into the mines straight from school.

I worked in Cilfynydd pit for 10, 11 years, then [when that closed in 1966] I worked in Merthyr Vale and I must have worked there for nine months, something like that, before the disaster. I never really liked it underground but, at that time, there wasn't much work about and there was good money in the pit so that's why I stuck the pit like. I was a collier. That's digging the coal out. I think the most I was working in was four-foot-six, and then the seam would go down to three foot, then four foot. Four foot was alright but it wasn't a great place to work; there was a lot of dust in them days. Later on they used to put water through the coal to stop the dust but it weren't so good in them days.

Your back was bent all day, shovelling, putting posts up, over the top. It was really hard work. You'd be on your hands and knees, sometimes all day when it went low – a fault in the ground, you know. And it would go lower, and you'd be digging it out with a puncher or a shovel. Sometimes the coal would be so hard, really hard. Oh, it would be murder, then, digging it. The puncher wouldn't get into it, and you'd be all day struggling to get your quota off. You'd have so many feet to take off, you had to dig in four foot, four-foot-six, and then 15, 20 yards, you'd have to take it all out. It was really hard work.

Miners lived with constant dirt and danger.

My best friend got killed in Cilfynydd. We grew up together. He was about 18 years of age. And another mate of mine at the top of the street, David Owen his name was... Oh, it was dangerous work. I had to dig one fellow out, a big slab come down and snapped his leg, pinned him down. We had to dig him out then, put a post under the slab and jack it up and drag him out of there. Oh, it was pretty dangerous.

Was I frightened? No, it don't enter your head, funnily enough. You got so much to do it just don't come into your head. But accidents, you know, regularly happen in the pit.

Hard graft and danger brought miners together in a special kind of comradeship.

I wasn't there long but the people there were marvellous, a real community, all stuck together.

That binding sense of community was evident elsewhere in the village. A source of strength in valley communities was their interlinking networks of extended families. Any child might have grandparents, aunts, uncles and cousins living nearby. Neighbours and family friends provided another cadre of 'aunties and uncles', and the street provided an informal family, especially for children whose natural playground at that time was outside the home. Chapel, choir, the pub and the club offered a further network of supportive friendships. Overlaying all of these, the egalitarian nature of Welsh society made for easy communication and mutual respect between social classes: teacher, collier and pit overman often lived in the same terrace of houses.

Gerald had moved to Aberfan from a nearby village when he married Shirley, a local girl.

I met my wife in Abercynon in a dancehall. I was 15 at the time. We loved to dance then. I won a competition jiving when I was younger, in Porthcawl, aye. There's a photo of us, it was in the local paper. 'Crazy Legs' they called her. She could dance! Jiving, Bill Haley, *Rock Around the Clock*, all that.

We got married when I was about 20. Before we got married we decided to buy this house at the bottom of the street because she'd lived in this street all her life. We bought the house and, of course, I was stony broke by then and so was she. Well, we moved in and were doing it up bit by bit like, you know. Every week we'd buy something for it when we could afford it and we were building the house up quietly like that. We were happy as sandboys, you know, in them days when we were first married.

My wife was a bugger for the kids. She'd have half the kids in from the school. They'd come and fetch their pets in, their mice and their hamsters and all that, you know. She loved kids. If she seen a kid outside the ice-cream van and he had no money, she'd give him a pound. Aye, she loved children. She spent hours and hours out the front with them kids.

Family life was paramount. The bond between parent and child was close but discipline was strict. Brothers Alan and Philip Thomas always knew when they'd gone too far.

Our mother could tell us off but she didn't have to say anything. It was in her eyes. She only had to give us a glance and we knew. She could look at us and her face would light up if it was funny, and if we were a little bit cruel – as boys were – you'll get a scowl and it was all done with the eyes.

She made sure we stayed safe, washed, dressed the same. For years my mother dressed me and Philip the same. If my Aunties were knitting and we had red jumpers, there'd be two red jumpers. There'd be two white shirts, two ties, two hats, two Burberry coats. What one had, we all of us had. There was always that love there, protection and love.

Children spent much of their childhood in the company of extended family, especially at holiday times. Porthcawl and the Gower peninsula on the nearby coast were favourite destinations for Jeff Edwards' family and for many others.

Weekends we'd spend with the family. We'd go on trips to the seaside, to Porthcawl, to Mumbles and Caswell Bay. We could go to the Brecon Beacons for picnics. Both my father and grandfather had a car. Sundays we'd spend with my mother's family. My mother liked to go to chapel at Pentrebach, not far from here and we'd spend the day with her family. So it was a close-knit family and a close-knit community and everybody was related to one another within the community itself.

For Karen Thomas it was the same. Her cousins were as close as siblings.

I'd got a brother and a sister. We were really, really close as a family. I remember we always went on holidays, two families – my Auntie and my Uncle and the children – we shared a caravan down in Porthcawl. We'd have our two weeks' annual holiday down there. And yes, we were quite a close family. In the community everybody knew everybody, we all knew each other. I think there'd be about 10 of us in the street and every day we'd be out playing, breaking windows with our balls! We'd play skipping; we'd have a big rope... As I say, we were a jolly community; it was a happy, close street.

Family times were valued by the Thomas brothers, as Alan recalls.

Fridays were always a special time in our house, especially the evenings. Mum would be at home, my Auntie would come up - her sister would come up from Aberfan from the family home and we'd have a lovely evening by the fire.

*

A visitor to the valleys in the 1960s would have noticed the tightly-packed nature of its villages: long terraces of small houses, front doors opening directly onto the pavement. Above them the oppressive blackness of the spoil tips with the sun rarely permeating the wet mist shrouding the valley floor and the pollution from the pit and hundreds of coal fires. But there was fundamental warmth to daily life. People lived rounded and fulfilling lives despite the constant risk of accidents underground and the lurking threat of closure to the pits that fed these tight communities.

Below ground men laboured and sweated to get the coal out. Above ground, evidence of mining was everywhere and accepted as an inevitable fact of life. Dirt, hooters, whistles and grinding lorries... and the tips. Mine spoil had to go somewhere as former Mines Rescue worker Malcolm Davies explains.

> When you dig a hole in the ground to sink a shaft, or drive a roadway into the hillside to extract coal, you get loads of debris. The rock etc has got to be dumped somewhere, it's not worth a penny. Unfortunately in the past coal owners and managers would dump that coal in the cheapest way possible, and the cheapest way would be as near to them as possible. They wouldn't want to carry it 10, 20, 100 miles away to dump it, and with our geography in the valleys - sloping sides - you just dumped the coal on the side of the valley, and of course when that tip was filled, they'd go on up further and tip the next one.

Like many others, Len Haggett saw that the valleys given over to mining were effectively appropriated by the NCB.

> From the Coal Board's point of view the mountains was regarded as a tipping area. You know, it was their land and they'd tip there.

The spoil after the washing of the coal was taken up the sides of the mountains to the tips by trams – small railways. A tram-track ran up the side of the school. Aberfan was surrounded by tips, built up over the life of the colliery, but one in particular dominated the village. Jeff Edwards, like everyone else in Aberfan, knew its history.

> Since the colliery opened in 1870, there were seven tips. And No. 7 tip, which was situated over a spring, a natural spring, was basically a huge tip that overshadowed the whole of the village of Aberfan.

But as far as the residents were concerned, the tips were an integral part of the landscape: they'd always been there and they always would be. Mary Davies didn't give them a thought.

In 1932, my aunt was married and I was bridesmaid. The wedding party had a photograph taken at the back of Moy Road and the garden was lovely... A few years ago I decided to have some copies made of these photographs and I went to the photographer in Merthyr. The first thing he said was 'Gosh, I didn't realise the tip was so tall', and it was, you know. You don't give it a thought when you're living with these things, do you?

Her next-door neighbour Mary Morse felt the same.

You'd go out into your garden and you'd look up and that slag tip was just looking down on you. You lived with it. We saw the trams going up there. It always used to be dirty where the Community Centre is now, there'd be stuff coming down. But I mean we lived with it. They wouldn't live with it today, which is a good thing.

Nevertheless No. 7 tip was a source of wonder for children like Alan Thomas.

But the tallest tip of all, and the only way I can explain the tallest one is – Mount Everest. It was a big top peak. And whether it was the material, or the sun from the summer, this rock used to get very hot, so we never knew for sure whether it was on fire inside, like a volcano, because when it drizzled in Aberfan or it rained, that one tip, the tallest of them all, would always steam. It would always look as if it was a volcano with smoke coming off it. So quite possibly it was on fire inside – we don't know. But as a child, it was awesome to see it smoking, you know. When I was in the junior school – two years difference between me and Phil – I used to look up at it when we were lining up to go into school and I used to think to myself, cor, that's high!

And its lower slopes were a tempting adventure playground.

> If you can imagine those tips, being a child, they were huge and I mean huge. I walked on them, I played on them. I got a row many times for getting dirty and getting holes in trousers... One of our favourite things were the leather conveyor belts that pulled the trams, carrying everything that went up that mountain. So we children, we'd go up there to play and if we were lucky enough to find a bit of leather belting, it was nothing for us to bend it up, up to our knees like a sleigh, one on the back, one on the front, and come down one of them tips. Drag it back up and have another go.

There were other games for everyone, girls and boys, down the generations, on the tip. Mary Morse remembers them from her own childhood more than 70 years ago.

> We used to have a bit of cardboard and slide down it and get filthy dirty. You didn't have a playground with slides then, so as children you thought that was wonderful. And then up by the tip... was a daisy field. That was right under the tip. We would love to go up there for a picnic. And then if you go further up there's a stream, but of course it was coming from under the tip, must have been. We'd paddle in that. Of course you'd have a row with your parents but we all did it, girls as well as boys. You felt safe, you know.

Sliding down the tip and playing in the stream that came from under it was mentioned by Gareth Jones and many others.

> When we used to go up onto the mountains, the slag heaps, there was always water running down them, and some people used to have blocks of bricks or whatever and damn it up, especially in the summer because

we weren't in school then... it was dirty water but to us it was fun.

Jeff Edwards too.

There were springs that came down the mountainside and fed into the canal. As kids we used to damn up those springs and paddle in them, looking for sticklebacks and tadpoles. We put them in jars, took them home and waited for them to become frogs, which horrified my mother as she hated frogs!

Everyone knew about the streams because everyone had played in them as children, so when the National Coal Board (NCB) denied any previous knowledge of them at the Tribunal Inquiry after the disaster, there was widespread disbelief. Bernard Thomas was among the unbelievers.

We played in the woods all round that area by tip No. 7, built dens and blocked up the stream. Coal Board said they didn't know the stream was there, but we knew about it. Used to dam it up, make a swimming pool, not far from the tip, and swim in it. The water was freezing cold. We'd get a bit of cardboard or something and slide down [the tips]. Of course we didn't realise the danger. You don't see it when you're a kid. It was a pretty popular area for playing.

Several of the boys, Len Haggett among them, would go up the tip 'picking' – looking for lumps of usable coal to take home or sell. This meant riding on the trams, a dangerous game.

I played on the tips as a youngster, you know, I gathered coal from the tips, I rode on the trams as we did in those days.

Daredevils like 13 year-old Calvin Hodkinson were prepared to resort to bribery to avoid parental disapproval.

> My brother Royston said to me, 'I know where you're going!' I said, 'We're going to meet some friends aren't we, Roy?' 'No', he said, 'I know where you're going, Calvin. You're going riding the trams. I'll tell Mam and Dad!' I said, 'You can't come, it's too dangerous. I'll tell you what I'll do. If you don't say nothing to Mam and Dad, I'll take you to the pictures Saturday, to watch the cartoons'. It was Batman and Robin at the picture house then. 'OK', he said, 'will you promise?'
>   So on that Friday I managed to ride the trams. I got a sack for the coal. It was dangerous. When the trams used to come down from the tip and we used to jump on, throw the coal off, and then jump back off, then collect it and sell it and go to the pictures.

There were other dangerous games. Gareth Jones and his friends used to play 'chicken' under the trams.

> You'd see a tram coming and I'd run under there and if you got splattered – the slurry was coming out, it would be slopping everywhere – you got caught, you see what I mean? That's what we used to do for fun in them days!

If children were aware of the dangers, they ignored them or revelled in the risks they posed because children then enjoyed a degree of individual freedom largely unknown today. Open ground began at the bottom of the garden and ended at the back gardens of the next valley. In every season the valley slopes provided a vast playground with the 'mountains' offering tempting woods, streams and ponds. There were still large pockets of natural beauty to enjoy. Mary Morse remembers picnics in what they called the Daisy Field.

Our mother would take us. And above there was the
Bluebell Wood. It was a very pretty wood with bluebells
in it, which is the A470 now. We'd play up there, Hide
and Seek, because in those days you could go up there.

Philip Thomas was often off in the woods behind their house in
Pleasant View on the edge of the village.

From school, I used to jump on the bus, go home and put
my playing clothes on. My mother would say, 'Tea, five
o'clock!' and I'd be up the woods. Where we used to live
there was no other houses, we were the last house in
Aberfan and then nothing but mountains. So I used to go
out with my bow, my arrow, my pellet-gun and shot
anything that moved! It was just the boys' thing. We used
to have sling-shots. My father would get up some
mornings and we'd cut the tongues out of his shoes –
there used to be murder then – just to make the old sling-
shot, out of wood, bit of wire, elastic and the tongue
out of his shoe. We used to have some rows for that!

Memories of young lives before the disaster are of freedom,
friendship and fun. Jeff Edwards remembers a happy, carefree
existence.

My friend David's family had a farm with a tree
plantation. We used to go up there, put a rope between
the trees and swing out into the forest. We didn't think of
the danger at all really, it was all just fun. When it was
harvest time and they used to cut the grass, we were out
till 10 or 11 o'clock at night and our parents had to come
up to the farm to pick us up.

As youngsters we had quite an adventurous life really,
an enjoyable one with all my friends. We used to go up on
the canal bank, on what was originally the old Glamorgan
Canal. We used to play on the tips themselves and between

the colliery and the tips. We used to slide down the tips on pieces of cardboard and it was all fun. But obviously it was a dangerous environment with these trams being full of spoil being pulled up to the tip-side. We were always shouted at by the men responsible for the haulage of trams up the mountainside.

We never told our parents we'd gone up there, as we would have had a row when we got home. So we kept that very quiet. But it was an adventure playground for us really. They were huge tips, 800 feet tall in many cases. No. 7 tip was right at the top of the mountainside so we never went up as far as that.

*

Parents might warn their children not to play on the tips, but few thought one would actually come down on the village. There were local concerns about the tips, but they were ignored by the NCB. Gerald Tarr remembers at least one petition.

There was an old fella in my street, just a couple of doors from me, and he even put in a complaint into the Council. There was a petition to the Council saying that tip is going to come down and kill us. 'My chest won't kill me. That tip'll kill me', he used to say. So they had that petition up there and what they done with it, they must've chucked it in the bin, because nothing was done about it. Nobody come down to see it. Few years after, it come down and killed everybody. When I moved into the street, they all said he was on about the tip. My wife knew everybody because she lived in that street all her life. She was saying the old fella kept saying that tip'll come down. We didn't take any notice. We were young and didn't realise, you know? But he could see it. The old fella could see it.

There were other concerns expressed locally that Bernard Thomas recalls.

> There'd been warnings to the engineers and the Coal Board... there was a petition. My Mam signed one. Of course they were dismissed as cranks. Basically ignored. 'Go back home and have a cup of tea', sort of thing.

There was hesitancy in official quarters about complaining too loudly about the tips. Some feared the pit closure programme might come to Merthyr Vale and so suck the life out of the village. Merthyr Borough Council, small and insignificant against the might of the NCB, certainly seemed reluctant to make a fuss. The area needed the mines so why take the risk when the tips had been there for decades, part of the landscape? Previous slides, one as recently as 1963, did little damage but were harbingers of what was to come. The warnings were ignored.

*

In the 1960s education in Wales was still the main route to self-improvement and a means of keeping brighter boys out of the pit. Teachers enjoyed professional status in the communities they served and solid school buildings fitted comfortably into local streetscapes. Pantglas Junior School was built in the traditional Victorian mould with classrooms off a central hall. Its Head Teacher Ann Jennings was in the traditional mould too, as Hettie Taylor, then a novice teacher, recalls.

> My first teaching job was at Aberfan. Miss Jennings took me in her car down to see Pantglas School. And it was a typical old-fashioned school, you know, with one big classroom to one side with three big windows in it, and everybody that was in there, the other staff, were lovely. They were so friendly, you know. They said, 'It's about time we had some young ones here'. I was 21.

It was obvious that Miss Jennings was in charge and she had a Deputy Head called Jack Evans who lived in Aberfan. She didn't always get her own way with Jack, he knew ways to get around her, but on the whole it was a really friendly school. There was Arthur Goldsworthy there, and Howell Williams, he'd started the year before me, so we had a good mixture of the older teachers and the younger ones. But Miss Jennings was a really good Head and she ran a tight ship. She wouldn't suffer fools easily but if she thought what you were doing was good for the school, she'd back you to the hilt. She had got that school just as she wanted it and the children respected her, the parents respected her and the staff respected her.

Hettie loved her job with the youngest junior class when she started there in 1965.

It was easy really, in Pantglas, because the children were, oh, they were superb, they were lovely. They listened, and I think because I was young, and the previous teachers had been that much older, they responded better. I did PE and I did Music, all things that they enjoyed then. The children were well-behaved. You had one or two that were... not naughty, wicked, you know (*laughs*). Alan Meredith wouldn't listen, he would get under the desk and keep popping up, you know. But they were lovely, and for me starting out, it was the best class I could have had, because they were quite a clever group of children.

And the children loved Pantglas. Jeff Edwards lived close to the school, in Aberfan Road.

The school was about 500 yards from where we lived. Each morning I would call on Robert, a friend of mine, the local GP's son, and we'd walk to school through the gulleys, which is what we in South Wales call the back lanes between the houses. In those days the surface of the lanes would be old coke thrown from the houses from the fire grates. The majority of houses had coal fires because the miners used to get coal free from the colliery. We used to call in at the little sweet shop not far from the school. Then at break time we had our third of a pint of milk too, in those days, with two McVitie's Rich Tea biscuits.

We enjoyed school. Lots and lots of friends, girls and boys. We played in the street or on the tip. It was always joyful, always fun. Mrs Jones was the teacher. The thing I remember about Mrs Jones was she had very red lips and she used to wear these little boots with astrakhan fur on the top of them. She was a dainty little lady and I was totally enamoured of her. She was very kind and caring and basically looked after us when we were in the Infants.

The school itself was Victorian, built at the turn of the century with a main corridor and a hall and classrooms off that. It had tall ceilings and teachers used blackboards and chalk not whiteboards like today. My teacher when the disaster happened was Michael Davies, who was a newly-qualified teacher. Miss Jennings was the Head Teacher. She was a lovely lady with white hair, and she was always a mother figure within the school, a very caring person. Hettie Taylor was the teacher in Standard One.

It was a nice learning environment. We were in Standard Two at the time of the disaster. I liked Geography – that's always been my passion, looking at pictures of foreign places and reading books about adventure. I enjoyed reading – the *Famous Five* and the *Secret Seven* – and we used to replicate their adventures, going up into the forests.

Alan Thomas went to the junior school and then on to the senior school next door when he was 11.

The school was always happy. I think that's the Welsh way. We were all the same, either your Dad worked in the colliery or in Hoovers... everybody was on a par, like. It was a fabulous place, I enjoyed school anyway. Never missed, always went to school right up to the time I was 15. It was a good social learning curve for your life. The teachers were lovely. They were like your special mothers, very thoughtful and caring. Jack Evans had the biggest pass in the Eleven Plus. He put a lot of children through – 14 or 15 children that year. He spent a lot of time with them, put a lot of effort in. Yes, it was a good school.

*

It seemed that nothing could dent the spirit or unity of this settled, rock-solid community. They knew who they were and were proud of it. They knew hardship, they lived with the pit and the dangers it posed, but work, family, friends and faith sustained them. It had always been that way and they believed it always would be. But the people of Aberfan would need all those qualities, all those supports - and more - to face what was to come.

2

AVALANCHE

No-one saw it coming. The morning was thick with wet fog in the valley, dulling sound as well as sight.

Someone mentioned they couldn't hear birds singing and it was true. It was like walking through a cloud in this thick, thick fog.

Aberfan was starting its day, like so many autumnal days in the valleys, in a damp blanket. So it was the noise that everyone remembers. Many thought it was a jet plane – 1960s airliners were as noisy as military planes, their thrust jet engines much louder than the dull whine of today's turbo-fans. Many hundreds of feet above the village the air was clear at the peak of tip No. 7 where the chargehand had noticed an unusually large sinkage movement at the start of his shift. Tipping was stopped.

But it was already too late. Around 9.15am a quarter of a million tons of mine waste, swollen by ground water and days of heavy rain, roared down the mountain, racing over a small farm and engulfing its farmhouse and killing the occupants. It carried on its merciless path, filling the old canal bed and breaching the railway embankment, rupturing two water mains in the process. Another few seconds and it struck the back wall of Pantglas Junior School, destroying the whole of the east side and filling its hall and classrooms with viscous black muck.

On it went, sweeping away a row of eight houses next to the school and cutting a swathe through more around the east end of Moy Road until it finally came to rest behind a terrace of houses a street below. The whole area lay under what the *South Wales Echo* at the time described as 'a black glacier'.

It had taken only minutes to change Aberfan forever.

It must have come down very, very quickly, like an express train. You couldn't see. You could hear, but you couldn't see what was coming.

*

For Hettie Taylor, class teacher to 35 six and seven year-olds at Pantglas School, the day had started like so many others.

I used to have a lift to school with a friend of mine who worked in Hoovers, the big factory in Merthyr there. And Michael [Davies] had just started in the school. He was among the very young teachers – it was my second year in the school – so Gerwyn used to come and pick us up. And I can see Michael now... he was sitting on the gate with a big smile on his face, waiting for us to come... In the car Michael was saying he wasn't having much success with reading [with his class], so I told him what I was doing with mine and he said he would try that.

When we came across on the mountain road – the new road to Merthyr wasn't built then – the mist was low and it was raining. That's typical of the valleys isn't it? As we came down into Aberfan it was all covered in mist. Gerwyn dropped us off. We got out of the car and Michael and I walked up to school, and on the hill going up to school there was always a lovely old man who used to come out and every morning he would say, 'Morning, Miss Taylor!' because he knew my name by then, and he'd say hello to Michael. People were friendly, they were like that.

Then we went in and Michael and I were still talking about reading and Miss Jennings came in [to the staffroom] and said, 'Right, it's time', and rang the bell. So we all went to our classrooms to meet the children coming in.

It was the last day of school, the children were excited because it was half term, we were going to break up. On the last day we didn't have assembly in the morning, we had assembly in the afternoon so's Miss Jennings could say to keep themselves safe, not to play on the railway, not to go by the river, and things like that. But the children were really excited.

Twelve year-old Alan Thomas was up early from his home in Pleasant View on the outskirts of the village.

Friday morning, as usual out on my paper round, first thing, six o'clock in the morning, up and out delivering papers for the local newsagent Terry Martin and Lionel, his father. My round at that time was Nixonville, Taff Street, Crescent Street, up to the park, back home. On Friday it was *Merthyr Express* day as well as the normal papers, so it took a little bit longer, I was a little bit late. Wasn't able to go back to the paper shop, so I decided to take the paper bag home. I arrived home for breakfast eight o'clock, Phil was getting ready for school. I had a wash, had my breakfast, and off we went. Double-decker bus. Bottom of the hill, got on the bus, upstairs straight away, everybody after the front seat to go to school. I was in the second class of Secondary Modern, and Philip was in the last class of Juniors.

Got down into Aberfan, just passing the Navigation Hotel, the paper shop was on the right, pressed the bell for the bus driver to slow down, so I could drop my paper bag off. As we were kids we used to just hang on to the bar, and drop off as the bus was still moving, we'd see how fast our legs would go... Got the paper bag in the doorway as the shop hadn't opened, and I started my way up to school then.

Alan's brother Phil, 10, had an easier start but was in school earlier, where he had an errand to run.

Got up as normal. Mum called us for breakfast. Me, my brother and my sister. More likely we'd have toast or porridge. Get ready then, with my brother, go down, catch the bus down the hill where we lived, on the bus to Aberfan. My brother used to have a paper round, used to jump off the bus to the shop to take his bag back, because his school didn't start till half-past nine. Then down off the bus and into school as normal, into the classroom, coats off, registration.

Then after that, one of the boys, Robert Jones, he owed some dinner money because it was half term and he owed a couple of weeks. Me and Robert went down then to the other school which is about 100 yards down the road to see his sister Margaret to get his dinner money that he owed. We were chatting to some children up on the wall by the gates of the senior school. It was a wet, very wet morning, couldn't see hardly anything in front of you, the mist was down. It was raining and it had been raining quite a lot that week. We were just standing talking, waiting.

Eight year-old Jeff Edwards was in the second junior class.

We were looking forward to half term, it was the last day before the holiday, so we were all excited. I picked up my friend Robert and Robert's mother always used to do Bovril sandwiches, which I hated. Robert was a bit late and his Mum asked us if we wanted these sandwiches so I said, 'No, thank you'.

We walked along the back lanes to the school and picked up a couple of sweets at the shop as usual. After registration ... I went to pick up a library book as I'd moved on from *Janet and John* by then, so I went to the shelf by the window nearest the tip and picked up from the shelf *Hergé's Adventures of TinTin* and walked back to my seat which was completely at the other side of the room and I was at the third desk up from the front. I sat down, and then Michael Davies the teacher started the first lesson which was Mathematics and he was chalking up on the board.

Bernard Thomas had a regular route to school.

We used to walk up the tip behind the house here, over the bridge, a few hundred yards through the cutting to the railway track and the canal tow-path, that's where you come out and then up to the school. Myself, my brother and few friends come along and we was talking on the way to school...

We went into class and were sitting down, reading a book. Middle of the classroom in a group of four or six desks, the teacher sort of behind me, the windows to my left. We got on with the activities we'd been given by the teacher, Mr. Williams. We couldn't see much [outside] for the fog.

It wasn't usual for parents in Aberfan to take their children to school then. Traffic was light and the school was relatively close. Older children looked after younger siblings and friends' children. Parents would wave them off to school from the doorstep. Seven year-old Karen Thomas started her day as usual, walking to school with her cousins Stephen and Angela.

My cousins lived six doors away, so I'd call for them, and my mother would stand by the door and the three of us left for school that morning with my Auntie and my other cousin [David] standing on the door. We walked to the bottom of the street and when we looked back we couldn't see them, because normally they could see us walking all the way through Moy Road. We could go to school on our own because there were no roads to cross or much traffic around and they could see us three-quarters of the way up Moy Road till we went to the dip up to the school and that's where they'd lose sight of us.

But that morning when we went to the bottom of the street we couldn't see them – it was very, very misty and foggy so the three of us turned round and we couldn't see them and we just carried on walking, laughing, the three of us. Got into school. I left Angela when we got to the school gates. We went up into the class, our classrooms were opposite each other, Stephen was the other side of the hall. We just parted company and went in our classrooms. And that was the last that I saw of them.

Karen's 11 year-old cousin David Hopkins, who she'd waved goodbye to on the doorstep, was at the senior school. He usually joined the younger children on their way to school, but not today.

It was quite a misty, kind of foggy day, and my mother, who was doing Home Helps, had the day off. I remember seeing my brother and my sister and my cousin Karen going to school but my mother wouldn't let me go with them. She had the day off and she wanted me to spend [a bit] more time with her.

Marilyn Brown waved off her daughter Janette.

She was 10. Sent her off to school that morning in the ordinary way. We had a son as well. Robert was six. And she would call for a little girl up the street, [Mary Morse's daughter Deborah] she was about the same age as Robert, and Janette would take them to school. Ordinary day. Went out to the door and waved them goodbye.

She wasn't very good that morning. She didn't want to go to school. And Bernard [my husband] was adamant, he said yes, and he had told her off a little bit. And she [*sigh*], she didn't want... it was trying it on really, you know what they are, they don't want to go to school sometimes. Sent her out of the door, watched them walking up the street. She turned around, waved. I waved back and that was that. Shut the door and came in and said to him, 'Good, we can have a nice cup of tea now, and I can have my breakfast'.

*

The village didn't keep nine-till-five working hours. The chip shop was open from early in the morning for men coming off night shift with no wife and dinner to go home to. Miner Gerald Tarr had had his dinner and was already in bed after a night's work.

We had a house, right down the end by the school, a row of eight houses and I lived on the end one. And then there was [the senior] school, just by the end of me there and the gulley going up, onto the mountain, up onto the bank. And I was on the end, sleeping. And this morning, I was laid in bed because the wife had just gone to work and I was working nights at the time. I was half-awake, half-asleep...

The chip shop had proved too much of a temptation for 13 year-old Calvin Hodkinson on his way to the senior school that morning.

My brother went off to school, he was in the Junior School and my sister was in the Infants. And that morning,

I don't know why, I was late. I loved going to school in those days, but that day I was late. But anyway I ended up with a couple of boys and the fish shop was open, Davey's Fish Bar, and they had pinball machines in there, so we nipped in there and had a few goes on the pinball machines.

*

In the Junior School Hettie Taylor and her class were just starting the day's lessons.

It was suddenly growing darker and we couldn't understand it. It was a rainy day and there was a mist going down so we thought, you know, it's just that. I think I'd finished marking the register and there was this terrible noise, like a growling noise, a dreadful noise. I started looking around – I couldn't see anything out of my window – I thought something had gone in the roof.

Bernard Thomas was in Howell Williams' class along the corridor.

All of a sudden this noise rumbling, rumbling, rumbling, and we didn't know what it was. I thought it was a jet plane or something. I was still sat in my desk. I looked towards the window and saw a wall of black. Slurry, like a tidal wave. And I thought, oh, that'll stop outside. But unfortunately it didn't.

The noise interrupted Jeff Edwards and the other children in Michael Davies' Maths lesson.

The next thing we were hearing was a sound like thunder and that gradually got louder and louder and the teacher

[was] trying to reassure us children, 'Don't worry, it's only thunder, it'll soon go'.

Karen Thomas wasn't in class. She'd gone with four other children to give their dinner money to the school meals clerk at her desk in the hall.

I was the last one at the table to pay the dinner money and while we were in the hall there was like a terrific noise and flying glass started coming down the corridor from the Headmistress's room. And Nansi Williams, the dinner lady – her reaction was very quick – she said to get on the floor on top of each other, but before even we could do that everything just caved in on top of us and she was on top of us. We didn't know what had happened. There was just this big noise and then the glass was flying from the Headmistress's room and then the wall from the classroom just seemed to fall and all of a sudden it was just there and we were buried.

Back in Bernard Thomas' classroom there was panic.

Pandemonium then, children rushing around and scream-ing. When it hit the school there was a tremendous crash-ing and next I felt being lifted up, desk, everything, pushed on top of the tidal wave. I didn't realise what was happen-ing, it was all black. I thought it was the end, basically. I was knocked unconscious for maybe seven minutes. There were rocks and stones and plants and trees and everything coming in.

As the slide hit the back of the school, in her classroom at the end of the corridor at the front, Hettie was increasingly alarmed.

I saw cracks appearing in the wall. And I thought, that's very strange, there must be something in the attic, and the cracks were getting bigger, it was quite frightening really and I didn't know what was going to happen so I said, 'Get underneath your desks, all of you. Stay underneath your desks.' And one little boy, Alan Meredith, wouldn't, he was always nosy, he kept popping up. So I went to Alan and held him under the desk and stood there.

The avalanche had by then engulfed Michael Davies' classroom. Jeff Edwards found himself trapped.

The next thing I remember was waking up with all this material on top of me. There were shouts and screams and 'Get me out of here'. I couldn't move at all because my desk was against my stomach and it really hurt. On my left-hand side there was a girl's head and that head was straight here, just next to my face really and I couldn't get away from it. The person had died and as time went on, her face became puffier. My right foot was stuck in the hot radiator, because my desk was against the wall nearest the hall and all this material was above me. All I could see was a small aperture of light and you could see through the roof – the roof had collapsed.

The screams then got less and less as time went on and I just couldn't move. I was stuck. It was a panicking kind of concern, and I really wanted to get away from this head. I knew the person had died. I didn't know what was happening. One minute I was in a Maths lesson, next there was all this. It was totally unreal.

Along the corridor, Bernard found himself on top of a pile of rubble and slurry.

When I came round, the first thing I remember was the other children, screaming for their lives, with fear... I could hear certain voices, crying for help. I thought, I don't know what's happened but I'd better get out. So, no broken bones, cuts and bruises, minor injuries. I sat up and looked around, I see my teacher and thought, if I can get across to there. I managed to scramble across the rubble, got across to my teacher and saw one or two children trapped like, partly covered, partly buried, some quite physically hurt as well. I remember my teacher pulling at his foot and helping me out – I'll have that memory always.

I saw the little panes of glass at the top of the classroom door were smashed through, so he helped me out through there and across the main hall of the school. To the left of the classroom there was a bank of slurry and the corridor to the right was blocked by slurry. But a couple of the main windows of the hall on the Moy Road side were open so I got across to there and got out of there. A chap helped me out and I found my brother – because his classroom was on the road side of the school and the caretaker had opened the window and helped his class out.

The school caretaker, Stephen Andrew, was the unsung hero of those first incomprehensible moments. He had opened up the school earlier to light the boiler and then gone to his home nearby at 77 Moy Road for breakfast. He was among the first on the scene after the slide hit, where one of his first actions was to kill the fire in the boiler. He had a responsibility to the school but more important, he knew his two sons, Malcolm eight and Kelvin 10, were inside. He went immediately to the remaining accessible windows on the front of the school where Hettie and her children were still in their classroom.

Then there was a knock at the window. It was Mr Andrew the caretaker and he said, 'Can you get out? Can you get out?' I had said to our children, 'You stay under the tables and the rest of them will come round and help us', not knowing at that stage what had happened. So I said, 'I'll have a look'. I went to the door and there was an iron girder through the glass and when I looked out, the corridor was like a tunnel. Things had come down but it looked as if there was a gap at the bottom. You could see a light at the other end, which was the outside door to the yard.

So I said to the children, 'Right now, listen now. You've got to go out. It's dark out there, but you must go straight out', because my corridor led to that door. So I said, 'Right, it's fire drill and you go straight out in the yard and stand still, don't go running around'. So I went to the door and, as I say, the girder was coming through, but Mr Andrew had come in by then. He pushed and I pulled and we managed to open the door. I said again to the children, 'We've got to go out now'.

We walked and crawled. Mr Andrew pulled the outside door open and I said to the children, 'Go and stand in the yard. It's fire drill. You stand, boys and girls, and no running around.' I went back in then to get the register, because I realised that when we did fire drill that was one thing Miss Jennings instilled in us, was that we took the register with us when we went out. So I went back, I got the register and went back out.

Her colleague Rene Williams' Reception class next door also had help from Stephen Andrew, as Gareth Jones, then five, recalls.

Nobody knew what was happening. Within seconds, everything seemed to go blank, quiet, nobody could hear nothing. But she got us up, out of the window, and the gentleman, the caretaker, he actually got us out of the school.

Further into the school where classrooms were full or filling up with slurry, Jeff was partially buried and still trapped at his desk but unlike many of his classmates buried or asphyxiated by the black slurry, he was at least able to breathe a little, but horror was very close.

The lucky thing about me was that I was in a pocket of air so I was able to breathe. I was gasping for air because it was getting less and less and I was panicking, thinking, how am I going to get out? The most distressing thing was this girl's head on my shoulder and my inability to get away from that. I used to have terrible nightmares for many, many years after, reliving the image of that person – the puffiness of the face, the eyes sunk in the head. It was very, very troubling.

In the hall, Karen and her four classmates were also trapped under a pile of slurry beneath the body of Nansi Williams who'd thrown herself over them when everything caved in around them.

We couldn't move. I remember just moving my arm a little bit. We were trying to claw at the stuff on top of us but you could only move your hands a little bit. You couldn't raise them up or anything because it was just all over us. We were just there, shouting and screaming at the dinner lady, trying to get a response off her, and just shouting out 'Help!' in case somebody could hear us. It was really, really dark. We didn't know what was on top of us, didn't have a clue.

After we'd been there quite a long time we told each other to shut up because we were tired and getting on each other's nerves shouting and crying. Between the shouting and crying because of being scared of the unknown, wondering what had happened and wondering whether we were going to get out, I think we were just exhausting ourselves. I think we were in an air pocket because we could breathe quite easily; I think we were in and out of consciousness through being there for so long.

Well, I just didn't think we were going to get out. I thought we were just going to be there until we stopped breathing. It was really scary. The dinner lady wasn't saying nothing to us, so I started pulling her hair with my finger-tips because I could feel her hair. And there was shouting, you know, the five of us were shouting, and there was no response off the dinner lady at all. We were calling out her name, we used to call her Mrs Williams, and the boys were saying, 'Just pull her hair if you can reach her', to try and wake her up. We just thought she was sleeping or unconscious. It didn't enter my head that she was dead on top of us.

*

Having retrieved her class register and gone back outside, Hettie looked back at what remained of the school.

I couldn't believe what I could see. Our end of the room was still standing but there was black behind where the other classrooms were. You couldn't see anything. It was as if the mountain was right up against the school, you know. I took the children down onto the road. I didn't know if I was doing the right or wrong thing but I just thought, 'You've got to get away from here'. I said, 'I want to you to run home, tell your Mams and Dads that something dreadful has happened in the school'. But I said, 'Don't look back, just run on home'. My children were first year juniors so it was alright for them to go home. And they did, they went.

Rene's class was next door. She was OK and her children were alright. So I went then to the other class-rooms to see if the other teachers were coming out, and when I came round the corner, it was just black. The back end of the school had all gone. By then slurry had come through and was coming out through the back door, so there was nothing we could do, we couldn't get inside. Outside, we really didn't know what to do. We were looking at the school and didn't know where to start. What do you do?

Gareth Jones was one of the younger ones who ran home.

> I'd only been gone 20 minutes from the house! I remember just walking in through the front door and of course I was stinking dirty. My mother said, 'Oh, what's the matter, what's the matter?' I said, 'Well, I dunno Mam, it's like the mountain's come down on the school'. She said, 'Don't be so daft! What's the matter with you?'

*

The destruction went wider; there was little of the east end of Moy Road still standing. Eleven year-old David Hopkins was late setting off for the senior school next door after his mother had kept him behind.

> I was walking towards school, going into Moy Road, when I heard this big crashing noise. I looked across and there was a nurse that lived across the road then and we both looked at each other. We went towards the noise and when we got there, there was... well it's hard to describe really, it was like the school was there, then it was all this rubble, then it was houses and then houses were gone, and there was some people coming out of their houses, because obviously it had just happened.

When the tip came down miner Gerald Tarr had been asleep at home in the end house of the terrace between the junior and senior schools.

> I had a big dog in them days, Buster we used to call him. Lovely old dog he were, but he never went upstairs... I was half-awake, half-asleep and I could hear the dog bounding up the stairs. With that he banged into the bedroom door, the door flew open and the dog run in. His ears were sticking straight up in the air and he was looking

at me. So I said, 'What's the matter boy, what's the matter with you?' And with that, the whole ceiling cracked straight open, all the way down and I thought, what the hell's happening here?

Then the back wall come down on top of me and squashed me down into the bed. I must have blacked out then because the next thing I realised, the house went down 50, 60 yards down the street, down the hill. I woke up buried alive.

Phil Thomas, sent on a dinner money errand with a classmate, had been chatting with friends outside the senior school.

We could hear a rumbling noise then. Sounded like a train going over a bridge, or a bulldozer. Then it was if someone was throwing stones at us, so we started to run. Robert went one way, back up towards our school, and I run the other way, down the road, there was a main road going down. I remember something hitting me on the back of the head. I went down, my hands came up, covering my head. Then just quiet and black.

Next thing then, I woke up, pitch black, couldn't see a thing. Crying. Screaming for my mother. I just wanted my mother, nothing else. Just that, shouting, screaming, 'Mam!' [*Upset*] Couldn't make no sense of it at all, it happened so quick. It must have come down very, very quickly, like an express train. You couldn't see. You could hear, but you couldn't see what was coming.

Marilyn Brown's friend Mary Morse had sent her daughter Deborah off that morning with Janette and was about to go up to Moy Road for coffee with another friend who had children close in age to her own. Pat Evans lived close to the school, in the same terrace as Gerald Tarr.

She had two children the same age as mine, a son aged six and a little baby. I had a son, a baby and Deborah who was five. Her husband was a teacher. Her son Hywel hadn't been very well all that week, he'd had bronchitis. He could have gone to school that day, but, like children are, last day before half term, he didn't want to go, so she said, 'Oh, I won't send him in'.

That morning Deborah had just gone off to school and I was putting Huw [the baby] – he was screaming – in the pram. I thought, I'd take him up to Pat's early, he'll go off to sleep and I'll get everything done. I went back to my kitchen, and I noticed he'd gone quiet, he'd fallen asleep. Oh, I thought, there's a chance now to do my breakfast dishes so I tidied up and I put the bin out.

If I'd gone when I should have gone, when he was crying, I would have walked just right into it. It saved my life really, him screaming. Fate? I don't know... I just missed it. I didn't see it. I was a very lucky person.

By the time she'd left the house for Pat's the tip had fallen and her daughter Deborah was on her way home, dirty and distressed. Next door neighbour Mary Davies heard her screams outside.

I was working part time in those days, and it was Friday morning when I usually did my cleaning. Then I was aware of screaming, and it didn't sound a natural scream, if you can call a scream natural, but something made me go to the front door, only to find Mary's daughter, Deborah, running up the street, still screaming her head off. I said, 'Oh what's the matter?' and she said 'The school has fallen down!' 'Oh' I said, 'don't be silly'. Then I looked beyond her, and I could see all the slurry, washing down Cottrell Street and I thought, my gosh, something has happened...

By then, Mary Morse had reached Moy Road and could see the devastation.

Well of course I went up, but what I saw, I see straight away there's nothing anyone could have done. The emergency services hadn't arrived by then. The men that did get up there were working on the front of the school but they weren't near the side entrance. The men had to climb over rubble to get to the front of the school to get anywhere, where the side entrance it wasn't so much – there was rubble there but they didn't have to climb over a hump of stuff, they could just move it away from the door and put it down away from the door and see if they could get in or if they could save anyone.

The area where I was, at the side entrance to the Infants, nobody was coming out. But what impressed me was, women – ordinary women like myself who I knew very well – just handing brick to brick to brick to each other and putting them down in the yard. Exactly like a conveyor belt. The women were in shock, you could see that in their faces. They were grey. I suppose we all looked like that... they were all in shock and not a word was spoken. I was really numbed, stunned. I don't know what I thought. Just could not believe it.

As far as Mary knew, Deborah was still somewhere in the school. It all looked hopeless but she and the other women felt they had to do something.

So I joined in the end, and got involved in the line of women, but I couldn't do much. Futile really. You know, there was nothing you could do...

Then she remembered her friend Pat.

This gentleman came towards me, this ex-teacher Jeff, I knew him because of the rugby club, and he said, 'Mary, are you alright?' and I said, 'Yes, but I'm going over to see Pat, to see how she is'. 'You can't go and see Pat', he said,

'Look'. And when I looked, I don't know, I went to pieces then because there was nothing but tree trunks and slurry – and she lived in a stone-built solid house. There was nothing there. Nothing at all there.

*

Phil Thomas, dazed and in shock, was buried in the avalanche of slurry down the hill from the school.

I didn't feel no pain whatsoever. Didn't even know what had hit me. I knew there was something wrong with my hand. I could feel my fingers were all squashy, I remember squeezing them when I was buried.

Meanwhile his brother Alan had been on the way to school.

I got as far as the Aberfan Hotel and noticed there were a lot of children starting to run home, some of them with no shoes on, dirty and wet. I shouted across the road, 'What's happened?' and one of the little girls shouted back, 'The school has collapsed'. I decided I had to get up there. I'd left Philip on the bus and my last words to him were, 'I'll see you later'. It was six to eight weeks before I seen him again.

Got up to the school, I couldn't believe what I was seeing. There was nothing there, it was black. The front of the school towards the road was intact but the back end where all the classrooms were, were in a mess. So, being 12 years of age, didn't know what to do.

We decided – there were quite a few of us by then – we'd go into the houses opposite and see what tools we could find. So that's what we done. 'Course the house I chose, there was a lady there – I can't remember her name – I asked, was there any tools we could use? There was a little boy in there, laid out on the floor. He'd been taken out but unfortunately he died later. He was alive, he was breathing very roughly, like. Obviously he had been crushed.

There wasn't any adults about because the night shift had gone to bed and the day shift had gone to work, either in the colliery or the Hoover factory. So I picked a hammer up and a couple of coal shovels, little hand shovels, and went off back to the school. Of course the only way in was up to the windows, we broke a few windows and in we went. They were big, high windows, like chapel windows, plenty of light. The only way in was to break the windows, break the frame and go through, which as a little gang we did.

My one thought was my brother. I needed to find him.

Also concerned for his younger brother was Calvin Hodkinson, who'd been detained by the pinball machines at the chip shop.

I think there was about three or four of us in Davey's Fish Bar so, we rushed up then to the school… there was police everywhere, people everywhere and… anyway, I think we started digging, and somebody came up to me and he said, 'Oh, your mother's looking for you, Calvin'. I said, 'Tell her I'm OK… I'm looking for Royston'. I was digging away and digging away and… I was in such a state at the time, I was only 13 like, so I stopped, I went home, to see my mother to tell her I was fine. She was crying in the house, she said, 'Where's Royston? [cries] I said, 'I don't know Mam, I'm going back now to look for him'.

Gerald Tarr was trapped, not in the ruins of his house, but under his bedroom door many yards down the road.

Being a miner, I realised I was buried. The bedroom door more or less saved my life. That bedroom door landed on my chest and shoulder, it crushed me down but it left me a breathing space on the bottom so I had a bit of air. Otherwise, if the door wasn't there, I would have had no air at all. It would have been all over my head and face.

I felt pain like, in my body and I started to shout for help. But nobody came. I lay there for a bit. It seemed like a month or two. I don't know how long it was but it seemed like forever. It wasn't all that long they told me after. But I was under there, tried to move my shoulder. No good. Started to pray to God, get me out of here like. At the end, I started to run out of air. I knew I was dying. My tongue started to swell, you know when you're dying. So I prayed to God to take me out of it because I was dying slowly.

*

The material that hit the school is usually described as slurry. In fact it was harder and heavier than that term suggests. Mining waste – slag or spoil – was a mix of coal dust and the worthless earth and rock that surrounded the coal seams. Normally it would have been dumped near the mine entrance and surface works. Aberfan's misfortune was that, in the absence of available ground on the valley floor near the mine, waste was tipped on the top of surrounding hills. Over the century of its existence the Merthyr Vale mine had already thrown up seven spoil tips. Tip No. 7, started in 1958, was only the most recent. Existing ground water and heavy rainfall made the tips inherently unstable – there had been two significant slides in 1944 and 1963. And the underground spring that provided a splashy playground for the children of Aberfan in the summer months was in constant danger of undermining the stability of tip No. 7.

Though many witnesses describe it as 'mud' – much of the surface of the slide in the immediate aftermath was still soaking wet – newsreel footage shows it as containing stones larger than bricks. By the time the avalanche came to rest just behind

Aberfan Road it had swept up large chunks of masonry, wood and metal from the buildings it had demolished in its path.

How the usually solid slag heap was transformed into a tidal wave of semi-liquid muck and rubble was explained in some detail in the later Tribunal Report. The spoil was kept in place by gravity and friction. The springs on which the spoil was knowingly dumped had been fed by exceptional rainfall. When mixed with coal dust, the water liquefied the spoil, reducing the stabilising friction and turning solids into something like wet cement. The resulting down-flow was powerful enough to dislodge the larger lumps of waste, turning a small shift into a full scale avalanche with immense kinetic energy.

No wonder there was no time for a warning or evacuation. It had all happened within minutes.

*

By now the tip had stopped its downward plunge but it was still unstable. The water that had liquefied it was slowly draining away down the gullies to the river, though on one side of the slide there was a new threat from the burst water mains gushing water into the street. People were gathering at the scene and the news – much of it scanty or garbled – was getting through to local emergency services. No-one was yet sure of the cause or the scale of the catastrophe, but there was no doubt that it was one. The following hours saw ordinary people in increasing numbers at their extraordinary best in desperate efforts to find survivors.

After the women's conveyor chain and the early efforts of the men and boys like Alan Thomas who'd arrived on the scene in the first half-hour, there was relief at the sound of heavy boots marching in unison up Aberfan Road. The day shift at Merthyr Vale had been called to the surface to assist. Many of them drilled by wartime and National Service, they knew that marching in step was the most efficient way for a body of men to get somewhere in a hurry.

It was an emotional moment for Hettie and it still causes tears.

> The next thing I remember was seeing the miners coming [*cries*]. Somehow or other they'd found out what had happened and they came straight off the shift so they came up with their helmets on and their lights on. They didn't run, they marched, and after they came, they took over. You know, they knew what to do. You got to remember that some of those miners had children in the school, but they knew that instead of just looking for their own child they had to help everybody, so they just went in regardless.

Medical student Mansel Aylward, visiting family in the village, had come to help. He remembers a moment 'not of sadness but exhilaration' when...

> ...suddenly, it was like the Seventh Cavalry had arrived because the lights came on on the site and I well remember these miners and the Mines Rescue people in yellow and orange with their steel helmets. And they came in as if they were the Seventh Cavalry and they started digging like people had never dug before.

June Vaughan was there with her husband Cyril, who had previously worked at the school.

> Before long a lot of local people arrived and the police arrived. We realised it was massive because of the look of the school. Then the miners from Merthyr Vale colliery came and they came with their headlights on. And I can remember thinking, it will be alright, they know how to rescue people. Everything's going to be fine.

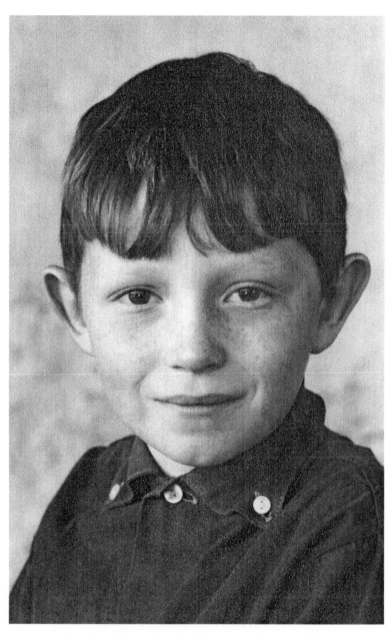

Calvin Hodkinson's brother Royston died in Pantglas School.

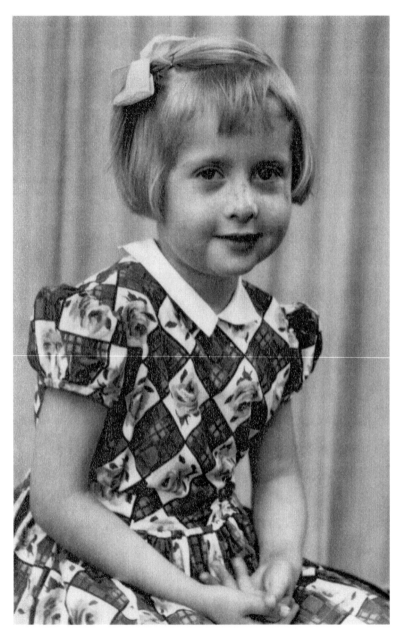

Marilyn Brown's daughter Janette didn't survive the disaster.

Brothers Phil and Alan Thomas, close from the start.

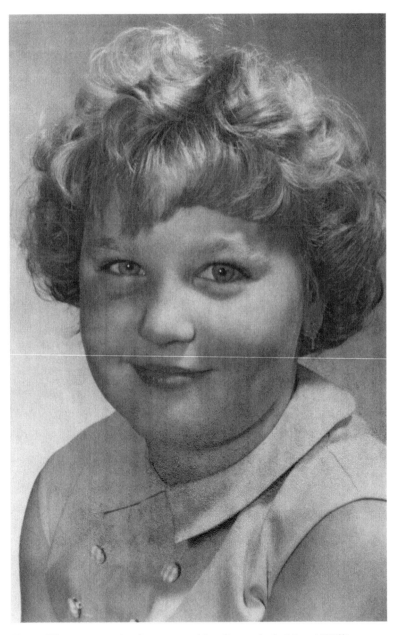

Karen Thomas survived, protected by dinner lady Nansi Williams.

Phil Thomas, 12, recovered from his injuries.

Karen Thomas (right) in a school play before the disaster.

Alan and Phil Thomas, growing up together.

Pantglas School staff Summer 1966: Hettie Taylor
(front left next to Miss Jennings), Howell Williams
(back left), Rene Williams (front right).

Aberfan Young Wives Keep Fit display: Mary Davies (back
left), Mary Morse (back right), Marilyn Brown (front right).

Dave Thomas, Station Officer Merthyr Fire Service in 1966.

Len Haggett (second right) with Fire Service colleagues.

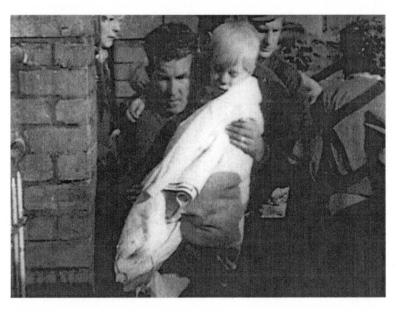

Jeff Edwards rescued from the school.

No 7 Tip, Aberfan. *Old Merthyr Tydfil*

Pantglas after the tip slide. *Old Merthyr Tydfil*

Volunteers form human chains to remove debris from the school.
Media Wales

Rescuers search for survivors. *Media Wales*

People from all over the country came to help. *Media Wales*

Jeff Edwards after the disaster, by Rapoport. *IC Rapoport*

3

RESCUE

The speed and the scale of the rescue effort still astonishes. But this was one of Aberfan's biggest problems. Very soon there were too many people at the scene trying to help. The first day was chaotic. For many of those directly involved, time became meaningless: they might have been there for minutes or for hours; it might have been morning or afternoon. There are some known fixed points but many of the accounts overlap and precise timings are elusive.

In fact the rescue began before emergency services and the miners arrived, when the tip hit the back wall of the school. Before they knew what was happening, bewildered teachers had managed to shepherd nearly half of the younger children out of the building to safety. Five year-old Gareth Jones was one of the 110 children saved this way and he will always be grateful to his teacher, Rene Williams.

> I was lucky to get out. I would really, really like to say a big thank you to my teacher. Even though she didn't know what was going on, that got us out alive. If she wasn't as quick as she was, no doubt it could have been a lot more. I've always said this, and I will always say this to the day I die... my teacher deserves an OBE or an MBE because it was her quick thinking that saved our lives.

The children were told to run home and tell their mothers. Some were not believed – until mothers saw the devastation for themselves. Then the word spread quickly. After seeing her daughter Janette off to school, Marilyn Brown was settling down to her breakfast.

Well, I don't think it was two minutes when Jeffrey, Bernard's nephew who was working for him at the time – he was a builder – came in through the back door, and he said something had happened to the school. I said, 'What?' He said, 'I don't know but you'd better come quick'. So I ran out the back door – I had an old pair of sandals on, an old jacket, to the next street. And the next street the water was pouring down the street, absolutely pouring down the street. The weather was awful, it wasn't a very nice day.

I got up to the school. And I just couldn't believe that part of the school had come down and my first thought was, oh, the children have already come out, they've had them out and they're keeping them somewhere. And someone said, 'No, the children are in there'. So we were waiting there. I said, 'What about Robert? Is Robert anywhere about?' 'Don't worry about Robert. Someone has taken him home'. As it happened he'd come out of one of the windows of the school and somebody had gone and looked after him. He had been told by a teacher, 'Go straight home. Don't look back. Go straight down the street and don't look back'. Which he did.

As more people arrived at the scene the first call to the emergency services was logged. It was just 9.25am. The first fire tender arrived five minutes later. At the time Len Haggett was a Junior Fire Officer with the Merthyr Fire Service. Like his fellow fire-fighters, Len had little inkling of the nature of the incident they'd been called to.

On that morning the alarms went off. I went down to the Watch Room and I was told a house had collapsed in

Moy Road, Aberfan. So I drove the emergency tender down to Aberfan.

When he arrived the scale of the tip obscured the school. All he could see was the devastation in Moy Road.

When we arrived in Moy Road – I'd lived in Aberfan – I realised that a complete row of houses had collapsed and right across the road there was a 20-25 foot wall of coal slurry. Initially I was not aware that the school was involved. We were dealing with rescues in Moy Road and we couldn't see over the slurry. Leading Fireman Bill Evans on the first appliance was there with me. We could hear people calling out from beneath the rubble.

Like the miners, the Mines Rescue Service had been alerted. These mainly former and serving miners were highly skilled at dealing with accidents – but underground not on the surface. Roy Hamer had been a mines rescuer for seven years at its base in Rhondda.

The bells went down at the Station and the first thing we do is we change in the van as we go along because, at that moment in time, we don't actually know where we're going. We're all changed and we're sat there in the van and the Assistant Superintendent at that time, Mr John Jones, I asks him, 'Where are we going, John?' 'Oh', he says, 'we're going up to some school in Merthyr'. And I always remember, I turned to the men in the van and I said, 'Gents, this is going to be something terrible. What the hell do they want the Mines Rescue Service at a school for?'

Malcolm Davies, Superintendent of Bryn Menim Rescue Station, was also called out.

All we heard over the radio was that Dinas [Station] is turning out to a school where there's been a tip slide.

There was no mention of casualties, there was no mention of anything else.

Mines rescuer Bob Griffiths was similarly bemused at first.

We ran over to the station, grabbed our bags out of the locker, threw them into the van and then we were on the road. We asked, 'Where is it? What is it?' and we were told: 'It's a school', and every man jack of us had to go, which was unusual because usually it was just a turnout crew of five or six men, the rest of them would be on standby. It started filtering through via our radios that a tip had slid into a school in Aberfan. Well, the first thing we said was, 'Where's Aberfan?' If they had said the village in Merthyr Vale colliery, we'd have known.

He soon discovered the scale of the challenge. The tip, full of water, was still moving.

On approaching I looked out of the window and the first impression I had was of a large diameter pipe, actually bobbing on the slurry from the tip, actually bobbing along as if it was a lump of timber on waves. Couldn't believe it.

For the first ten minutes we were moving stuff out of the way, to see if we could find any casualties. It was a lot of people doing a lot of digging at the time, basically with their hands. We were digging with our hands because we didn't have any tools on the van - they were equipped with breathing apparatus not with tools for digging.

No-one dared think who or how many lay under the rubble. Marilyn Brown was still staring at the devastation in disbelief while her husband Bernard joined in the digging.

There were quite a lot of people there by this time... Quite a few of the women were onto the heap, the old part of the school, passing bricks and stones, and it didn't seem real somehow. I thought the children must be out of the building, they must be somewhere. They can't be in the school. I didn't realise how bad it was, I really didn't. I must have been dreaming or in denial, because I didn't want to think that they were still in that school and I think a lot of people felt the same way. Everybody's faces were so grave and so worried.

Unbelievably, children were among those digging on the tip. Disobeying his mother, 13 year-old Calvin Hodkinson had gone back to look for his brother Royston. He didn't find him, but he did manage to effect a rescue.

I was digging away with my hands... all of a sudden I can see a hand. I shouted to the workmen, 'Quick, there's somebody over here!' They said to me, 'You've done well. Move away now'. It was a little girl they had out of there, and she was alive.

Eleven year-old David Hopkins had seen his two younger siblings off to school that morning. Now the school had gone. He went in with another boy to help get children out.

We didn't go in through the doors, we went in through the windows, because the windows were all broken, and we tried to help children out. We weren't in there long because somebody just said, 'Get out! It's not safe! Get out, it's going to collapse, everybody come out!' I can remember there was a girl covered in muck and bleeding a little bit, and somebody told me to take her home, so I took her home. She lived down one of the side streets... I think it was only then, I was in the street and it kind of hit me, my brother and my sister... and I think I started to cry then, suddenly realising that they were up there.

Using tools borrowed from nearby houses, 12 year-old Alan Thomas and his friends had managed to get into the school through the windows before the emergency services arrived. He was looking for his brother.

> Where we entered was the hall where the assemblies were held. The classrooms were then facing you. There was rubble in the hall, stone and brick, because it was an old stone building. You could hear some little outbursts and cries and you realised that there was somebody underneath.
>
> Fortunately one of the adults with us was a bus-driver. He couldn't get his bus through the village and had come up to find out what had happened. We started moving some of the rubble but some of it was too big for us. He moved it and I believe he got a little girl out.
>
> I knew exactly where Philip's classroom was, but it wasn't there. It was one of those classrooms that had really caught the brunt of the tip. You know when you lose something that's precious to you? You keep looking and looking and you keep thinking, where would it be? It was a case of what do I do next? Was he in a different class?
>
> Systematically, we broke every window we could, and systematically we found nothing. Every time we opened a classroom or took the windows out, there was nothing there – it was just a black canvass from the ceiling to the door. And it was still moving because of the water that was running through it. It was just unbelievable how it kept moving. How long for I don't know. In a child's eye five minutes could be an hour and an hour could be a day.

Alan was in a highly unstable ruin and the tip had not yet run its course, but he was determined to find Philip.

> My concern was finding my brother and I didn't think of the danger. I never thought of anything falling on me.

It could have quite easily. I could have moved something. I could have opened a door, dislodged something and anything could have fallen on me. Your natural instinct was that he's your brother. You were brought up together, played together, fought together, cried together, ate ice cream together. Your mother wiped your faces together. You're inside a living hell and you don't see the danger.

I had to get back out of the school. I went through the cloakroom where all the coats were still hanging. There was light coming through, picking out the falling dust and it looked like lots of little stars coming down.

By this time, women had come from the village and they were organising themselves and passing stones out. Somebody must have started organising them or maybe it was just human nature. The whistle was sounding on the colliery and apparently the miners had started coming up.

In fact the first miners had arrived in their own transport, but word had spread fast and the day shift was soon called to the surface to assist at the school. Bare hands were no match for the weight of the slurry – as soon as they removed debris, more took its place. So the miners' arrival – with the Mines Rescue men fast behind them - was greeted with great relief. The miners had the equipment and they knew what to do; they commanded everyone's respect, as fireman Len Haggett recalls.

If you're ever asked what resources would you want in an incident of that nature, we had the best in the world. We had the miners. They were the boys who could shift the slurry, who could support the roof and who could continue to search to see if there was rescues.

Len was about to be involved in two dramatic rescues of his own. Alan Thomas was looking for Phil in the ruins of the school, but he wasn't there. He'd been swept by the avalanche from the street outside the senior school into Moy Road where he was trapped, half-buried.

> I was shoutin', screamin' and I could hear voices, people digging. I heard someone saying 'There's someone here!' They dug me out and as they lifted, I realised there was a bedroom wall on top of me. I remember the wallpaper. They got it off and lifted me out.

Phil's rescue – not straightforward in itself – coincided with a flood of water from the two ruptured mains between the old railway embankment and the canal bed behind the school. Len was part of the small team trying to get Phil out from under the wall.

> A young boy was trapped beneath a wall and he was trapped by his feet. Though we could get at his head and shoulders we just couldn't get him out. Other people came and one of them was Dave Thomas, Station Officer in charge of Fire Prevention in Merthyr – my boss. And there were probably about six or seven people around this stone trying to lift it but not succeeding. And then the inrush of water started and you could hear the people calling, 'The water's coming!'
> And the water was coming. It was coming in and around this young lad and we had to hold his head up, back out of the water that was coming. And we done one last effort – something had to happen – he had to come out, damaged, hurt, but come out he was going to have to come. And we done one final lift and how we lifted that wall up I don't know, but we did. We raised it just long enough to get our arms around his shoulders. And as they lifted, we pulled and he came out. If he hadn't come out, within a few minutes he would have drowned.

Dave Thomas had joined them to help.

All you could see really was the upper part of his body, from the shoulders up, because the rest of him was covered with slurry and all the timber and everything that was being washed down, at such speed it was still moving then as well. He was obviously in agony. Well [it was a] race against time because the slurry kept coming down like a river, and he had to be got out of there as quickly as possible, otherwise he would have been covered over.

Seriously injured, Phil was as close then to death as he could have been.

I thought I was going to drown. But they pulled me back out of the water. Then I must have gone blank for a little bit.

When he came to, he was in an ambulance on his way to St Tydfil's hospital in Merthyr. It was a sweet moment for Len and Dave.

It was a feeling of elation then, that we had saved a life. That this boy had been able to be pulled out of there... We had to hold his head back out of the water and he was terrified, understandably, and I was afraid we were not going to be able to get him out. But we made that one last effort and out he came. And that was elation, without a shadow of a doubt.

But there was another casualty buried in the slurry and rubble of the ruined Moy Road houses who desperately needed their help. Gerald Tarr, trapped under a door, was running out of air and convinced he was about to die. He was praying to go quickly when he heard a familiar voice. It was Llewellyn, his milkman.

Of course I was screaming my lungs out but he couldn't hear me. I thought, I can hear him, why can't he hear me?

I thought I was shouting, but I wasn't. But he must have heard something because he dug down onto my stomach, chucking the rubble away. I could feel the air come to me. Oh, it was something out of this world! It was like someone put a hosepipe full of air blasting into me, it was cold, freezing cold you know? And now I could take a breath. Llewellyn was looking for his son at the time and he told the firemen, 'Come and dig this guy out!' Two came up and started to dig.

One of them was Len Haggett.

We had to remove all the material that was on him and the door. We couldn't actually remove the door completely... Because we didn't know what his injuries was, we kept talking to him all the time. We were concentrating on getting him out and you were aware that there were other people within the houses that you could hear. But you could only deal with the rescue that you were doing. You had no equipment that was any use to you. It was just a case of attempting to pull the stones away and the material that was on him, trying to get a sufficient space that we could get him out.

But there were other hazards to come for Gerald.

They dug my head out and part of my body but they couldn't get my shoulder and my arm out because they were the other side of the door. As they began digging, a big slab started sliding down. It was like the side of a house, about a ton in weight probably. So the fireman said, 'We'll have to stop digging'. Oh God, what are they going to do now? 'Go for the jacks!' he said to another fella.

In the meantime, this other fella came up. 'Get him out of there – 'the pipe has burst. If you don't get him out now he's going to drown!' Cor! So I was clawing at that hole, trying to get my shoulder out from under the door. I thought, 'I'm not going to drown now after all this!' I was clawing away, taking my fingernails away, clawing at this door.

Finally the firemen come up with jacks and lifted the door. With that, this doctor came down into the hole. He scrambled down, putting himself in danger because if this slab had have gone, he would have gone. He came down and put a jab into me. They still couldn't get me out because my shoulder was down under this door. But they come up with some sort of a scissors jack or something and the door went up six, seven inches, and they dragged me out of there.

I thought, thank God for that, I'm not going to drown. They said to me, 'Can you stand?' I said, 'Oh, aye'. I tried to get up, I couldn't get up. I thought my back was broke, you know? My back wasn't broke, it was my pelvis was broke and of course this was all crushed in, I was bruised from head to foot, I had no skin on my head, all my skin was gone, as if someone had scalped me.

They chucked me on a blanket then, and rushed me to the ambulance. There was a policeman in the ambulance and he was smoking. I said, 'You haven't got a fag have you?' I couldn't have smoked anything anyway because my jaw was like this [*jaw moving up and down, lips trembling with shock*]. 'No, I don't smoke', he said!

*

While rescues were being valiantly attempted and the injured dispatched to local hospitals, all was chaos at the disaster scene. The school building was in a dangerous condition with its roof hanging unsupported at one end, the slide was still unstable and the inundation of water from the two burst mains was jeopardising the rescue operation.

On the other side of the water, at the school site, hundreds of people were digging, trying to remove larger pieces of debris, looking for anyone who might still be alive, with hundreds more standing by, shocked, helpless or simply fascinated by the extraordinary scene. The village itself was clogged with traffic and emergency vehicles, with the two main access roads to the site blocked either by the slide or by the torrent of water still flowing from the mains. A BBC radio newsflash at 10.30am had brought in hundreds of offers of help, medical assistance, goods – and more people. Emergency workers like Malcolm Davies had to be diverted to help control the traffic and the crowds.

> We weren't aware of anybody in charge, so that all the people that turned up to the school, they were trying to get in to get to the children... and that was the problem with the whole operation, the Mines Rescue would have been in charge underground and your Colliery Manager would have been directing operations, but because there was nobody in charge, everybody was trying to do their own thing... Anyhow, I was asked by I don't know who, if I could possibly try to get people away from the site, because there were hundreds of people arriving in Aberfan to assist.

Mansel Aylward, driving to Merthyr for a family baptism, had been stopped by a policeman at Dowlais Top and told to find another route because of the disaster. But then the policeman noticed a British Medical Students Association badge on the car windscreen.

> He said, 'Are you a doctor?' I said, 'No, I'm not a doctor, I'm in my final year'. He said, 'Well, I think you'd be useful in getting down to Aberfan'. He knew I had relatives there and we had a short chat. Then I realised it was the school...
> ...I had great difficulty getting into Aberfan because having to cross the bridge which goes across the river to

get into Aberfan from Merthyr, there was slurry on the road about a mile or so before getting to Aberfan. But I drove through it – and broke my axle on the car! Then I had to walk. And when I got up into the site I didn't expect to see what I saw. The slurry, the coverage of the houses, many of which had been just taken away – and then the school. And they knew I wasn't a doctor, so they said, 'Well, give us a hand. We're going to examine the kids as they come out and get them off [to hospital] as soon as possible'.

Alongside the continuing frantic rescue efforts, work was now being done to help secure the site. Here the miners came into their own, as fireman Len Haggett observed.

I always admired their skills – in the sense that the roof was hanging down, it was dangerous. Yet they came and the repairers as they called them looked at it, grabbed a length of timber, wet it with his thumb and said to his mate, 'Saw that'. And he did and it went up perfectly. And that occurred a number of times. No measuring tapes, no nothing. Just look at it and assessed what length he wanted, where it was to go and it went. And this is what was going on to protect the people who were still working in that area to try and find children and to make it reasonably safe – and this is what they done. And though everyone was heroes that were there that day, members of the public, everybody else, the miners were probably the best men you could have had at that scene.

Mines Rescue man Roy Hamer knew how the miners worked.

Previously there was no pattern to it. Now there would be continuity, the whole area would be covered and nowhere would be missed out. What would happen is that you'd have a Rescue man there probably with five or six miners in a little area and they would work their way through, and that would be for the length of the school as they would work the way through exactly as they would a seam of coal. They were slow, but progress, obviously. There was no-one as efficient as them in digging out slurry. You'd be confident that nothing would be left behind.

Progress was being made but there were still many children trapped in the school. Some estimated 150. Having successfully evacuated their classes, teachers Hettie Taylor and her colleague Rene Williams were on hand to offer what help they could.

Rene and I were just outside then, and you just wanted to go in and help, but the miners wouldn't let us go inside. So we drew a few maps and told them where the class-rooms were, but you could see the back end of the school, there was nothing there. And they started then, bringing children out. I don't really know how they did it, digging gently I suppose. They'd blow a whistle and call for silence. Then you'd hear a shout, 'There's one here!'

Everyone remembers that whistle and the call for silence: it could mean another child might be saved – or that another body was found. For fireman Len Haggett it is a painful memory.

Even within the school they'd be working and suddenly you'd hear a whistle blow and they'd say 'Silence!' And it's incredible, with all the people there, you'd have abso-lute silence, hoping that you could hear a voice. And then the whistle would blow again and they would continue.

And that went on, and on, and on. But how you could obtain silence in those circumstances with that number of people who were present is difficult to imagine and yet it was. You got absolute silence, hoping that you would hear a voice or a call so you could rescue them. [*Breaks down*] It's emotional, I'm sorry.

And it was emotional at the time, even for many of the rescue workers. Malcolm Davies recalls seeing a part-time rescue man he'd worked with at the Rhymney Valley Station years before.

He was a miner, an official overman underground, but he was Polish, he'd come from Poland as a youngster. His English was perfect and he was a charming chap. But he was standing near the entrance of the school and some were shovelling, some were passing out rocks and boulders and what have you and he was struggling with a shovel, but the tears were running from his eyes.

Hope was high but no-one knew how many might still be alive. Karen Thomas, delivering her dinner money in the hall, had been protected with four other children by the lifeless body of Nansi Williams. They were starting to think they would never be rescued.

Then I felt something hit me on my shoulder – obviously they were starting to move the rubble away – and I screamed and we all started screaming and we could hear digging and somebody say, 'There's someone here!' 'Yes, we're here, five of us, come and get us!' we were shouting, and all of a sudden I could see daylight. So we knew then that we were going to get out, but until that point we didn't even know that anybody was looking for us.

When we looked up all we could see was these men and when you got out you were like passed from one to another like a chain. My Mam said we came out about 10 to 11, so it's probably from about 20 past nine... I remember being pulled out. I remember having a little cream leather purse. There was a penny in there for me to go down to the tuck, because I wanted to have a drink. I was very thirsty, and I had a lot of black stuff in my mouth that they were trying to clean out, but they wouldn't give us anything, they wouldn't allow us to have anything. I was asking, 'Where was Angela? Where was Stephen?' And she was saying, 'Don't worry about them now, you're on your way to hospital. They'll be OK'.

For Hettie, seeing children brought out alive was an emotional experience.

At one point they brought out another child, you could see it was a little girl, with blonde hair, very, very pale. It was Karen Thomas who I'd had the year before. She was very badly injured but the doctors said they were certain they'd be able to help her and she was going make a recovery. And she did because she came back into my class.

A lot of the children who were handed over to us were badly injured from the weight of the slurry on them and they didn't know what had happened to them - they were in shock. But to see a familiar face, someone they knew, must have helped them. One or two would smile and say, 'Oh, Miss'. Some of them didn't talk at all, some of them were unconscious, but it was so wonderful to see if somebody's eyes moved, it was fantastic, you know.

Jeff Edwards was still trapped under his desk in Michael Davies' classroom. He was in an air pocket but was suffering the horror of being stuck, unable to move, next to a dead classmate. In a class where so many had already died, Jeff was extraordinarily lucky.

I had very white hair so I was easy to spot. The firemen started to dig into the rubble around me. They also started to remove the fallen roof beams and the desks that were on top of the rubble. They got down to my desk itself and they just couldn't shift it because of all the stuff that was around it. So they got their hatchets out and actually broke up the desks. I remember I'd bought these felt tip pens in the newsagents in the village – they were sixpence each and I had four of these pens so that was near enough two bob in those days. I said to them, 'Let me get my felt pens, I don't want to go without my felt pens'. And the fireman said. 'Bugger your felt pens, let's get you out of here'.

Then I was thrown in a human chain from one fireman to another, on to the volunteers, through the classroom, into the hall and then out into the yard. It was chaos really; there were people everywhere, anxious, waiting to see whether their child had been recovered. We were examined by medics out in the yard and given an injection, of what I don't know, wrapped up in a blanket and taken off to the local hospital.

By the time I got out, all the ambulances had gone and Tom Harding, who was the local greengrocer in the village, he actually carried me to his van, which was parked in the lane, not far from the school. There's a picture of me from one of the old black and white films showing Tom Harding carrying me, with my mother at his side. I remember he had a blue Bedford Commer van, and there was water rushing down the lane. He couldn't start the engine because the water was going up the exhaust. But then eventually it started and I was taken up to hospital in Merthyr Tydfil.

But at approximately 11am, Jeff was the last to be brought out alive. His mother Tessie remembers his shocked reaction as they hurried to Harding's van.

He kept saying all the time, 'Oh, she was dead, see Mammy, she was dead'. *All* the time. And I'd say, 'Oh no, she's sleeping', trying to calm him down. But it wasn't. She'd died.

Lifeless bodies were already starting to be recovered. These were some of the most difficult experiences for those, like Hettie, at the scene.

To begin with, the victims just looked as if they were sleeping. They must have been killed by the dust or the lack of air in the classrooms, or something like that... I brought out one little boy and I thought he would make it, but he was gone. And he was perfect.

Alan Thomas was still there looking for his brother.

I was still looking round and I just went from the back of the school but there was nothing, just a black mass. The school roof had all caved in and there was nothing, you couldn't get in anywhere, well, not at my age anyway. Somebody must have had one of the little girls out, and she was on the floor. I did know the girl and I spoke to her. I put my coat round her because she looked cold... But she wasn't alive [*upset*].

Unaware that Phil was already on his way to hospital, Alan finally decided he needed to find his mother, but the water was still flowing full-tilt from the mains.

I thought it was time to head home. I hadn't thought of my mother, hadn't given it a thought. My concern was Phil, I couldn't find him. I had to go home and tell her.

So I started off and I got to the dip in Moy Road where what we call the gulleys or the alleyways, where you could walk through... these gulleys went all the way down to the river. And of course the water main had gone, the tip had taken the water main out, so there was excess water flowing through that area, it was like a river going through. And I thought to myself, how am I going to get across this? I didn't know how deep it was, it was flowing water.

I was looking at it and when my head come up, my mother was the other side. I can see her now, she had her scarf on, tied underneath in a bow, that was the fashion.

Glasses on. Coat on and everything... [*Pause, upset*] My first words to her were, 'Mam, I can't find Philip'. And she walked straight through it. Couldn't believe it. Like she walked on water, she just come straight through it, she didn't hesitate. Caught hold of me, clutched me, I said the school had collapsed, because we didn't know what had happened. We didn't know it was the tip till after, when all the reports started coming in. That's all I knew: half the school had gone.

It took me about thirty years to realise, my mother sent two children to school that day – as far as she was concerned she had two sons in it [the disaster]. And when she seen me that morning and I was the other side of that water, her first instinct was: I got one of them. And she come through it. How she done that I will never ever know, 'cos my mother was never a big person – the height of her life I think she was only eight stone. So for her to do that, the strength and depth of her love must have been phenomenal. The protectiveness of it, you know, like an animal protects its pups, my mother had that natural instinct. That no matter who it was or what it was, or where it was, as long as we were safe, she would make sure we stayed safe.

*

The steady methodical work of the miners was paying off. Their extraordinary effectiveness meant that by 11am all those buried but still alive had been located, pulled out and taken to a makeshift triage unit where they received first aid. By this time 22 children and five adults – including Phil, Gerald, Karen and Jeff – had been taken to St Tydfil's Hospital. Another nine casualties went to East Glamorgan. Though both hospitals were standing by and equipped to receive dozens more, there were no more to come. The only casualties after Jeff Edwards were rescue workers injured by their efforts on the site.

The emergency services were soon augmented by Civil Defence and Salvation Army volunteers, both well used to supporting workers and victims in disaster areas. By midday, both water mains had finally been shut off and the last of the excess water flowed down the gulleys into the River Taff. The flood of volunteers however continued unabated throughout the day and into the next: university students, soldiers on leave, men and women from nearby factories. They came from all over the country, some prepared, many not, but all anxious to help. Mines Rescue worker Bob Griffiths recalls a librarian from Cheshire...

... a weedy little fella and he was initially up there shovelling and I said, 'You don't want to be by there, son, you're not built for this type of thing'. I called on the Salvation Army and they put him down in the clothing store.

His colleague Malcolm Davies helped equip the ill-prepared.

There was a group of young people from Northampton, they'd come to help which is marvellous, you know, you've got to take your hat off to people who would travel to try and help. But some of them were dressed – I wouldn't say high heels – but in flimsy shoes and a dress and they weren't equipped to help, so we gave them wellingtons, helmet, cap lamp and a shovel before we sent them up the mountainside.

At around 2pm, a command post was established in Merthyr Tydfil police station. Its task was to co-ordinate the rescue efforts at the school with the hospital and all the other sources of help on offer, including private haulage contractors and the armed services.

Everyone was working with uncertainty and, despite the skills and training of many of those involved, much of the response was improvised. No-one was sure how many were still missing, much less what the final death toll would be. But what permeates the experience of those there on the day is the instinctive compassion they observed from both local people and the complete strangers who'd come into the village to help – from those digging to the volunteers supporting them with refreshments and comfort for the bereaved. Overriding all the chaos and improvisation was the very best of human nature.

*

After taking part in the rescues of Phil Thomas and Gerald Tarr, Len Haggett had moved on to the school site. Here he'd helped rescue a young girl, but to his everlasting regret, she was his last. The remaining children he dealt with were dead. All this was happening often in full view of the parents. The recovery of bodies had to be handled with thought and compassion for those waiting anxiously for news.

> I was handed one of the children out through a window to take up to the Infants section which was being used as a temporary mortuary. The child unfortunately had died. But the gentleman alongside me was Dr Arthur Jones who was my doctor and who I knew fairly well. And as I carried this child up, Dr Jones was walking alongside and saying 'Talk to her, Len. Talk to her. We can't let the parents know'. [*Emotional*] And that's what we did.

Inside the school in the slurry-filled classrooms the sights were harrowing, even for the most professional rescue workers like Len.

> We went through the school, seeing if we could do any more rescues. And we realised we couldn't. When you see a teacher pinned against a wall... standing up, pinned against the wall among the debris in classrooms with the children around... [*upset*] it's a bit overwhelming.

Medical student Mansel Aylward had arrived to help the doctors.

> The first experience I had was one of the most distressing. I went into this classroom and there was this teacher with his arms outstretched and behind him were all the children. And all the children were dead. The sight was awful in the real meaning of the word because they'd all died of suffocation. My job was to see if there was anybody still alive but I was quite certain that there weren't.

Former miner and part-time fireman Allan Lewis had left his factory in nearby Treorchy to volunteer at the site.

> All I'd seen on the news was that children were trapped. I'd been a collier. I was used to shovelling. I just wanted to get there...

Allan worked from the afternoon well into the first evening in one of the most difficult locations, a slurry-filled classroom

> You can picture the classroom with the desks. There were little girls and they were all still sitting in their desks and the tip was sliding down over them... So our jobs, the six of us, was just shovelling it back... and we was just advancing slowly. But very slowly because of the amount of muck that was sliding down. There was tons and tons above us. And the people above us had got to be higher than the actual roof. The roof had been taken off completely.
>
> I helped to dig four little girls out and the schoolteacher. What I found hard to understand was how the room was so full of mud. The classroom door was only like four yards away and the teacher was on the side by the cupboard, the little girls still sitting in their desks. How they didn't have time for them or the teacher to escape or at

least for one of the little girls nearest the door to even make a run for the door... from what I could see, it must have come in like a tidal wave, took the whole roof completely off and just flopped down on them, filled the classroom with mud and they was buried within seconds I should imagine because not one of them made it to the door, which was only yards away... It was just like dragging them out of a muddy pond, the muck on them. Like little ragdolls, they was soaking wet.

The recovery of these bodies had been harrowing enough, but one of the victims struck a painful chord with Allan.

The little girl that I dug out then, I had a daughter at the time, four year old, and she had a pony-tail and this one I dug out was very similar to her with a pony-tail. The resemblance was there and she reminded me of my daughter, so I filled up then. I did break down, I started crying and the tears ran down my cheeks. The overman who was behind me said, 'Do you want to be relieved?' I took a deep breath then. 'No, no, I'll carry on'.

For Mines Rescue worker Roy Hamer, there was some small comfort in the midst of such chaos and tragedy.

The children were found all over the place because they were carried by the slurry. They were all over the place, desks, cupboards, anything... The only consolation when I look back on it, was that the slurry was so small and fine and it came at such a speed that I like to think that they suffocated straight away rather than suffered agonies. I honestly believe that that slurry was travelling at a rate and once it come into that school it swept through the school and the damage was done very quickly. I don't think the children were badly injured. The main causes were suffocation.

By 5pm that afternoon 20 bodies had been recovered; by 10pm 40 more. Initially the dead had been laid out in the Infants classroom. Hettie and Rene wanted to do what they could.

We thought we'd help by identifying them so that when the parents came – and by then parents had come to the school – we could save them having to look at a row of children and pick out their own child, which I would have thought would be a dreadful thing to have to do. So we identified them. The police had arrived by then and were asking parents to identify their children, and that was a terrible, terrible time.

*

After a day of searching and worrying, Alan Thomas and his parents still didn't know where Philip was. After meeting up with his mother, Alan was sent to his grandmother's while his parents continued the search, but he was restless.

I couldn't stay in the house... Friday evening and then of course, dark evenings, don't know what time it is, I made my way up to the canal bank which is beside the school. And I looked down over the school. The arc lights were on, and they were working. Every so often the whistle would go and everybody would go quiet. Then a shout would go up and they would start working again. This went on for hours. I spent at least an hour [there], maybe longer I don't know. My parents came and found me again, took me back to the house, still hadn't mentioned Philip.

In fact, by this time his parents knew that he was in hospital critically ill, but they decided not to tell Alan in case he didn't pull through.

The emptiness started taking over then, the emptiness and the loss. Where is he? I spent that night at my grandparents.

3 RESCUE

I was in my Auntie's room – my Auntie Glad who always came up on a Friday night. I was small enough to get up on the window ledge and I sat in the window and I watched the cafe and the fish shop working away, serving food, hot water, to all the workers who were coming down from the tip and it was unbelievable, the amount of people that were around...

Well I must have sat in that window for another hour, when I thought, I must get back up to the school. I was gone, like a whippet. Phil, Phil. Where is he? I didn't think he was dead, didn't pass my mind. It was just the thought, is he still in there? Is someone going to pull him out? It's just one of those things you can't explain, you know. He's your brother. What can you do? You love him [*cries*].

*

The heroic rescue phase was all too short-lived – little more than 100 precious minutes from the tip falling at 9.15am to the last rescue at 11am. The recovery phase of the disaster would last much longer – over a week. By the end of Friday 21st the death toll was still uncertain. Only once the last bodies had been recovered could the mechanical diggers begin the mammoth task of removing the thousands of tons of tip waste, slurry and detritus. But 'recovery' was the least appropriate way of describing what happened next.

4

COUNTING THE COST

In the immediate days after the disaster all was still chaos and confusion. Though the frantic rescue efforts of the first day were reluctantly giving way to recovery operations, the overwhelming influx of an estimated 2000 volunteers hampered progress and the village was choked with workers, vehicles, press and television crews. Of the surviving children, some lay critically ill in local hospitals, unaware of what had happened to them or of the fate of so many of their classmates. Bereaved families, drawn close for comfort, had hardly begun coming to terms with their loss. Others yet to know they were bereaved still held tight onto hope.

Marilyn Brown and her husband Bernard had waited for much of the first day for news of their 10 year-old daughter, Janette. Their young son Robert had already escaped from the school and was being looked after by a friend.

> We lived quite near the school. Time was passing and we were still wondering what was happening. We still didn't know what was happening. Then eventually news came through that quite a few of the children had been buried. This time we didn't want any more news. We were still thinking, yes, she'll be alright, she'll be fine.
>
> But no, eventually my father came down and he said that quite a lot of the children had been killed within the school. I said, 'Is Janette alright?' and he said,

'I don't know yet. I'll go and find her for you'. Bernard went with him.

By this time of course the children had been brought out and taken to a little local chapel so they had to go and identify the children. So my father and Bernard went to identify Janette. They wouldn't let me go. Afterwards, I thought to myself, I wish I'd gone. They came back home, and my father started to cry, and he said, 'Janette has died'. He'd just identified her. And I said, 'Oh, I want to go. I want to go and see her!' 'No', he said, 'you don't want to go and see her. She's fine'. I said, 'What does she look like? He said, 'She's got a tiny mark on her forehead, and she looks as if she's sleeping. That's all you've got to know'. But I did regret it. I would have wanted to see her.

And that was that. I just give in to it then. I cried and cried and I collapsed. I realised then that it was over. But all I wanted then was Robert. I said, 'Where's Robert? I want him near me'. And somebody said, 'He's not very far, he's in Auntie Mary's'. We always called her Auntie, she was a good friend. They brought him down and I wouldn't let him go. I wouldn't let him go for a long time. Bernard said, 'Let him go, Marilyn. You're holding on to him for grim death'.

I didn't cry then, funnily enough. I just wanted to hold him. From then on I can't remember anything else. Whatever people said to me, I didn't hear. I was in another world I think.

The people of Aberfan were temporarily suspended in a daze of grief and incomprehension while the streets vibrated to the continuous rumble of heavy trucks hauling tip waste away from the desecration of Pantglas School and the ruins of surrounding homes. By the end of Saturday 22nd, after a day of increasing rain and concerns about the stability of the tip, 118 bodies had been recovered and removed to the temporary mortuary at

Bethania Chapel where the police were in charge of the identification process, assisted by the Salvation Army.

Family friend Mary Morse had gone to the Chapel with Marilyn's father to identify Janette's body.

> It lives with you. I'd seen death before but not what I saw up there. Some didn't have a mark on them. I never speak about what I saw in the chapel. I wouldn't speak about that at all. But I thought I was helping Marilyn by doing it, and helping her father, because he wasn't a young man.

Salvation Army volunteers Dorothy Burns and Sheila Davies were at the door of the chapel, helping parents as they came in to identify their children. Dorothy found it an almost unbearably upsetting task.

> I think it was Sheila said to me, 'If you're going to cry now, you'll be of no help'. And you pull yourself together then, don't you? But it was the seeing of those parents' and families' face, it was awful.

Medical student Mansel Aylward was also sent there to help parents.

> And then I was asked to do something which is probably the most distressing part, and that was to take the parents of the children to a morgue that had been set up in a local chapel where they'd laid out children, helping to identify the kids. And that was enormously distressing, but I was able to do it. And that is the image that mostly comes back to me when I think of that time.
>
> Many of the parents that I met had either been in school with me, or I knew of them or their family because my family lived in Aberfan and it was just my job to help them go through that distressing period and to take them to their children, and support what the Salvation Army

was doing largely. It was very quiet in the chapel itself. Many were crying, many were just dumbstruck and didn't know what to do or how to think.

And then later in the evening some of the parents who had been through this terrible ordeal, they were breaking down six or seven hours later and I went to several houses they lived in in Aberfan, visiting them there, and, as I said, several of them were school friends of mine. So I had no experience, I was just a medical student, I just did what any normal person would try to do to comfort them. No medical issues, but now, of course I know the sort of thing I was doing was very important. I was talking to them, helping them to get this thing off their chest.

Teacher Hettie Taylor had initially helped identify the children in the Infants classroom, then in the chapel.

We were taken – I think it was the Chief of Police – to the Bethania Chapel and that was not a nice sight. They had the children on the seats and people were coming to the chapel now to look for their children. We went round and identified the children that were there, so that the parents only had to come and see the one child, not go through rows of children.

That Friday morning Hettie had shared a lift to school with her young colleague Michael Davies. He had just started teaching that autumn term and their last conversation in the staff room had been about reading schemes. Now she found herself having to identify his body.

They said they'd found a boy from the secondary school – because he was in his uniform, grey trousers and a blazer. Well, I knew Michael had come to work with grey trousers and a blazer on, and he was young so he could well have looked like a boy from the secondary school.

So I said, 'Well, I think it might be one of our staff'. So I went to see Michael and he was perfect. I don't think there was a mark on him. Absolutely perfect. But he'd died. So he was in his grey trousers and his black blazer but he'd died with his children in his classroom. And the sad thing about that was, that went through my mind, was his mother had said, 'Oh, I'm so pleased Michael is teaching', because his brother was a fireman, his next brother then was an electrician underground and Michael had gone into teaching, which was the safe job. [*Emotional*] But Michael didn't make it.

*

Salvation Army volunteer Sheila Davies had already had a full day serving tea to rescue workers on the first day.

We had this big yellowy orange urn that we carried around, two of you had to carry it because it was such a big thing. I don't know what possessed us, actually, to go around with this big urn, but we did.

On the other end of the urn was her friend and fellow-Salvationist Dorothy Burns.

We even carried a tea urn halfway up the tip! How we did it I don't know, carried paper cups under our arms and took the tea up. And that tea, you know, it brought something to them.

Their efforts didn't go unnoticed and unappreciated as Mines Rescue man Bob Griffiths recalls.

When you have two women – and not young women, you know, in their 30s – carrying a big urn up the mountain, to the tips so that the boys up top who were working to secure the safety of the people working below, carrying an urn of tea up there for them to have a drink of tea, those are the people, the Salvation Army volunteers, I admire the most. Not me. That was my duty. They didn't have to do it, but they did it when men refused to do it, so I was told, but they had no hesitation whatsoever.

Their voluntary efforts continued for many days after that.

Then on the Saturday we came back down early in the morning and the police had opened an empty shop for us on Aberfan Road, and in that shop all suppliers came with paper cups and plates, Sunblest bread, you don't hear of that today, but that was there then. All these people came, Cadburys, all first aid stuff came into us as well, gas bottles were put on, and we started making sandwiches to take out. It was remarkable how kind people were, and generous. It really was. They just turned up and dropped all the stuff off up at our shop... so from nothing, we had a main source of getting out to the people.

In fact, Aberfan was soon swamped with unsolicited donations of everything from soap and bandages to a gift of 60,000 cigarettes from Players. According to one account, even the prostitutes of Cardiff's red light district offered their services free to the rescue men.

Food was one commodity never in short supply. Dorothy and a small army of women volunteers made sure no-one went hungry.

Another thing we did, on the lorries that were continually going around Aberfan, there was like a tread place on a lorry, we would make sandwiches in a bag, step onto it – they slowed down – to give the drivers the packages so they could have something to eat as they were driving.

They were soon going into homes to take food and drink to bereaved families.

I think they were in shock, they were devastated. I don't think they realised what had happened. When we went into the houses there was a dreadful stillness there, you know, it was there. Some of those families hadn't eaten. They didn't think of eating any food, so we went to homes that had lost loved ones, and we chatted to them as well. I think we just went to comfort them, to see if they needed anything, and that we were there if they needed anybody to speak to... I think they talked to us more than what we talked to them, their feelings... How do you talk to someone that's lost a child? That's very, very difficult.

There were more distinguished visitors to come in those homes. In common with other bereaved parents, Marilyn Brown had to cope with a novel intrusion.

People were coming into the home. I do remember Lord Snowden coming and George Thomas [*Minister of State for Wales*], he came and they were very good, they were lovely. One thing I do remember is Vicky, my sister, was out in the kitchen, and I went out to fetch her. I said, 'Come into the other room', I said, 'Lord Snowden is there'. 'Oh Marilyn, don't be silly!' But she did and she said [to him], 'Oh, would you like a cup of tea?', like you would, like the Welsh people would.

Welshman Tony Armstrong-Jones, the Earl of Snowdon, husband of Princess Margaret and the father of two young children himself, was in the vanguard of distinguished visitors, arriving in the early hours of Saturday morning from his London home at Kensington Palace after hearing the news on the radio. For much of the following day he both received and made many cups of tea as he went into people's homes, his empathy and informality commented on by those he visited. Prime Minister Harold Wilson had made a brief reconnaissance visit to the site the previous evening and the Duke of Edinburgh arrived the following morning. Prince Philip returned, accompanied by the Queen, on October 29th. Medical student Mansel Aylward was nearby and was able to observe her from close quarters.

> I... wasn't very far from her. And she was visibly moved. Other people have said this but she was. You could see by her body movements, by her facial features. I didn't see her actually cry tears, but I felt as if she was crying.

In hospital Jeff Edwards, the last child to be pulled from the rubble alive, and his fellow survivors also had visits.

> Lord Snowden came... I was colouring in a colouring book and he came round to me and he actually drew a captain on the bridge of the ship. We had Alan Taylor who was a TV personality who came along with some of his puppets and tried to brighten our lives a little bit.

Some children were too ill to receive the early visitors. Ten year-old Phil Thomas, rescued from the slurry and then the mains water deluge in Moy Road, had been taken initially to St Tydfil's.

> I went to school that day, long trousers, jumper. The jumper had all gone, there was only a little bit left. My trousers had gone, just the belt left, the leather belt. [They] started cutting what clothes I had left off me. I remember seeing them washing me down. The more they washed, the more I bled. Then the doctor said, 'Stop washing, we'll take him into theatre as he is'. The muck and the slurry caked on me, formed another skin. And I went into theatre and next I knew then it was evening

time. Up on the ward years ago they used to have, instead of the curtains around the bed, it was the old screens on wheels. They were around me. In and out of consciousness, you know, I could hear other children on the ward.

Phil had head injuries and a fractured pelvis and was later transferred from St Tydfil's to the Prince of Wales Hospital in Cardiff. Though he remembers nothing of that initial period, the thought of the worry it must have caused his parents is still painful.

They kept me heavily sedated through my healing process. Dad said they were by my bedside the whole time, but I don't remember. It was, they tell me, 50:50 whether I would live or die. [*Upset*] It's... so, that's all I remember, seeing my Mum and Dad at the foot of my bed.

Karen Thomas, seven, was also critically injured.

I had internal bleeding so when I went into the hospital they had to remove my right kidney. So I lost my kidney and I was very traumatised. They said my whole body had closed down, it just shut down. There were seven of us in the ward. The doors of the ward were closed all the time, there was nobody allowed in, and that ward was known as the Aberfan ward. I never went out of the ward. My Mum and Dad never left the hospital for a week really.

Teacher Hettie Taylor was a frequent visitor to the children, for her the only bright spot in a particularly difficult time.

After, we went to the hospitals to see them. And it was lovely to think that some of them had survived such a dreadful thing and they still had a little smile on their faces for you, that was fantastic. They were wonderful, they must have realised how bad it was, but they were still cheerful. Some of them were seriously ill and it took a while before they were talking, and things like that, you know. But when you saw some of them that were fine, talking, it was wonderful.

In time, even Phil Thomas was able to receive Hettie with a smile.

I definitely saw him in hospital. He was full of it! [*Laughs*] He was one of those children who always had something to say. A laugh, a joke, you know. And when he was in hospital he was still the same. It hadn't crushed him, he was still Philip.

*

Among the 36 injured in hospital were more than a dozen adults. Miner Gerald Tarr was one. He had gone to bed after his night shift at Merthyr Vale only to be dragged some time later from beneath a door hundreds of yards from his destroyed home.

I went to bed just with my shirt on and by the time I got to the hospital I only got two arms and a bit of a collar. I was more or less naked. And this doctor said to me, 'Where's the pain?' I said, 'All over. From my head to my toes'. I was battered like. I felt like I'd been in a washing machine.

'So where's the worst pain?' I said, 'By 'ere' – where I'd got crushed – 'and by 'ere'. So he took me down X-Ray and I thought it was my back because I couldn't move. Well my back was injured like but, 'Your back is alright', he says, 'it's your pelvis that's broke, that's why you can't move your legs', he said. 'And', he said, 'you've got crushing to the shoulder and the chest. That'll take a bit to heal up'.

But I was in a fair bit of shock. My bottom jaw was trembling up and down banging my front teeth you know. I said I need something for that. A jab or something, I don't know what he give me. That seemed to slow me down like.

My wife came in the next day. She was with the next door neighbour's wife. She wasn't looking for me, she was looking for her husband. Of course her husband was dead and this bloody fool was still alive. Someone must have told her I got dug out. She couldn't get up till the following day, traffic jams everywhere they tell me and the place was in chaos, getting the children out, you know.

At the time they had to put my pyjamas on frontwards because my chest had swollen right up and I couldn't move my arm at all. So of course I was in a bit of a state in the bed when my wife come in. Because my hair was all full of rubbish and matted like, no skin on my forehead, my pyjamas only just frontways.

She looked at my chest in the area where the bedroom door crushed me – it's a good thing it did mind, or I wouldn't be here today. She started to cry and one thing and another. I said, 'Look, stop crying. I'll be alright now. Don't be crying about me, love', I said, 'I'm happy just to be living', I said, 'I'm happy I'm not dead'. You know, because I should have been.

One of his rescuers, fireman Len Haggett, was still at work after his initial rescue and recovery efforts on that long first day.

For a couple of days after the disaster I was in the police Control Room in Merthyr with Dave Thomas. We were acting as liaison officers because that would be the main Control Room. I went back down to Aberfan on a number of occasions because the feeling of the community was such that it was felt that we should base a fire engine in

Aberfan with a crew permanently for that time. So I went down and formed part of that crew that was based in Aberfan.

One job was particularly sensitive.

I went down later when the houses in Moy Road were being removed by JCB diggers and I went there to supervise and monitor the removal of the houses because there were still people who were unaccounted for. So every time the digger bucket was tipped in the lorry it was tipped slowly so that we could see what the contents were before a further one went.

It was a difficult job because you were hoping you were not going to find what you were looking for. And that was the persons who were remaining within the houses. But it is something that you had to do and yes, you would look at each bucket and get it dropped slowly, slowly, slowly, so the contents could be seen. And you would have a sigh when you didn't find anything you were looking for. So it was traumatic, but it was something that had to be done.

The recovery of bodies was dealt with by professionals like Len and the men of the Mines Rescue Service. They took a necessarily detached approach to their gruesome work. Bob Griffiths was used to dealing with fatalities.

Unfortunately I didn't handle anybody that came out alive... When I started in the Mines Rescue an old rescue-man once told me, 'You will have to deal with casualties, and possibly bodies'. He said, 'If you come across a body, treat him with respect but don't think of him as a body, think of him as a piece of wood. Otherwise', he said, 'you're not going to be able to do this job'. So you don't actually think, at the time, of a body as a human being, it's only later on when you're away from the area, that you start thinking about things. At the time you just don't. That was the best piece of advice I ever was given. You've just got to detach yourself, otherwise you'll go mental, you just won't cope.

But the strain on the men carrying out recovery work must have been intense. Roy Hamer led a small team from the Rhondda Mines Rescue Service.

I suppose I could say we were used to it. The same things would happen but they would be happening underground with adults, which was a different ballgame altogether. We'd go into places like Cambrian [*a 1965 mine explosion killed 31 miners*] and Tower [*a 1962 mine explosion killed nine*], wherever there were explosions there were obviously very nasty little areas, if I can put it that way. It was the same there, the only difference is you're dealing with children not adults and that's the biggest difference of them all.

I was rostered to go back there on the Saturday evening, Sunday morning. And it was a terrible night. The rain, the winds – whatever it was weather-wise, we had it. And by then they'd only partly erected the lighting, very poor lighting, the tip was still on the move and from time to time a great 14-inch pipe would come floating down the tip on top of the slurry. So we all had to be very aware of what we were about.

I had a team of men with me and probably it must have been about two or three o'clock in the morning when all of a sudden nobody was talking and, from experience in rescue work, if no-one's talking you've got problems. They'd all had enough. You're dealing with children rather than men. That's what got at everybody. And I've got no doubt in my mind that, for the first time – and I hope the last time – it certainly got at us that night. You'd be there shovelling, whatever, carefully doing these things and then you'd come across a somebody or a something and you'd just pass it on to be taken away. But they'd be children and that's what gets you.

We were afraid to look at one another and I was beginning to wonder what to do. It had obviously got at us. So I said to the men, 'Come on, let's go and get a cup of soup'. Now by this time they'd put up little soup stalls about 50 yards apart and we all went over to one of these soup stalls and I think we were all like zombies then. Several police had already gathered there and there was this young lad, probably about 12 years of age, and he was serving out this soup.

So, you could imagine, the police had all lined up and the first person to have his cup filled was the Inspector. So this young lad, he's going down the line filling their cups. With that, the Inspector finished his soup and he stepped forward to help himself and this lad shouted, '*You bloody do that again and I'll book you!*'

Now, can you imagine this, with the atmosphere that was there then? We all burst into laughter, and what made it more hilarious was the police standing by, they were afraid to laugh at the Inspector weren't they? Well, you can just imagine what we, the workmen, made of that. Afraid to laugh, are you boys?

But God bless him, that little lad didn't realise what he'd done. He had given us the punch, the trigger, call it what you like, to stir us out of our pitfall. We drank our soup, and went back into the quagmire different people until the end of the shift. But really, it wasn't us saving the children, it was the young lad saving us. That was the truth of the matter because at that time we were hopeless – before that little incident that put us right back on our way.

After Jeff Edwards at 11am on that first morning, no-one had been rescued from the site alive. Professionals like Roy and the many volunteers toiled on regardless, more in hope than expectation.

> Obviously we were always motivated by hope, and the men would look to us because of our status as Mines Rescue men. We were always in hope, perhaps for the first week even, always looking for that little miracle that could have happened perhaps. As we know now, there were no little miracles.

Despite their professionalism, they could not help but be affected. Former miner and part-time fireman Allan Lewis recovered the bodies of four little girls and their teacher from the school.

> It was a very sad time and a terrible, terrible experience. It's awful hard to explain... You try not to have any feelings when you're digging these girls out, but when one resembles your daughter you can't help but feeling, what if this was my child? You can't help feeling for the parents, waiting for this child to be dug out... I'd rather not think about it to be honest with you. I try to put that part out of my mind if I can.

Denise Morgan, who lost her sister Annette, remembers that slim hope being finally extinguished and the effect it had on her.

> My father had been looking for my sister since the Friday morning really, and then on the Friday evening, he came back home and he said 'I still haven't found her yet, but, we're not going to give up hope, we're going to try and find her.' So I think at that point we felt, oh, alright, there is a bit of hope, but in the morning then I can remember him coming back in through the door, and just presenting my mother with this piece of material, and saying, 'Is this what she wore that morning to school?,' and my mother

just looked and she went, 'Yes, that's it, that's her dress.' And I can remember it now, it was pink, pink and red and flowery, and there was quite a piece of it there, and that's when we realised then, that it was her, in the mortuary.

I had this feeling of this overwhelming emotion and unable to say... to grasp it. I mean she'd left that morning, we'd slept together the night before in our bed, and all of a sudden she wasn't coming back anymore, and I remember the first night I went to bed after – on my own obviously – I kept saying to my mother, 'I can't breathe, I can't breathe,' and she kept coming back and forward into the room and I said, 'I can't breathe.' But I think it was just the situation I was in really, at the time. Just feeling overwhelmed by it all.

*

Though the number of suspected dead had earlier approached 200, the unofficial death toll closed at 144 on October 28th when the final unaccounted-for body was recovered.

The previous day a short mass funeral for 82 of the dead, 81 of them children, was held in Aberfan's Bryntaf cemetery, an event captured from a respectful distance by television cameras and shown across the world. A procession of funeral cars bearing small coffins and a giant cross formed of hundreds of wreaths were visible from across the valley. One individual floral tribute was a model of Pantglas School.

This was the emotional nadir of the disaster and the event interviewees found most difficult to talk about. Given the extraordinary scale of the funerals, attendance was restricted and all those who attended had to have official permits. Even so, there were conditions placed on bereaved families too which must have caused additional distress to grieving parents. Salvation Army volunteer Sheila Davies had been handing out refreshments to the rescue workers, but she and her husband were given another job in advance of the funerals.

The thing that really, really sticks in my mind is two or three parties of us, I think Trevor and I were the only Salvationists, we were given five houses to visit, and we had instructions to tell them about the funeral, and the fact that there wasn't room for all the family to stand around the grave as you would normally do, and you had to sort of say you'll have to work it out for yourselves, who should be nearest and who wouldn't. That was the saddest part for me, having to tell them only certain people can come and stand around the grave because you can't take up somebody else's room.

I'll never forget one lady coming to the door and her husband just behind her, and her face was red with crying and we went in and she said she had adopted this little girl, and she didn't want to go to school that morning, because it was the morning before half term, and she'd persuaded her that she should go and the holiday would be the next day. And she said, 'We had no happiness until she came, and we have no happiness now she's gone'. And that's something that really sticks in your mind.

After that, she was too upset to go to the funerals.

I couldn't go... it just seemed to drain everything that I'd got. I sat at home and watched it on the television, and then hearing the drum just playing the beat as they walked along, then that's when I started to cry, and realised the enormity of it all.

Children were kept away from the funerals. Karen Thomas's 11 year-old cousin David Hopkins lost a brother and sister in the disaster.

I was sent away for the funeral. My Mam and Dad didn't want me around. No, that's the wrong words. They just didn't want me to be there, to go through it all. I was sent to my Auntie's.

Jeff Edwards, sufficiently recovered to be discharged from hospital, was staying with his grandmother.

> I found it very, very difficult to go back to the village because I was afraid of the tip coming down again so I spent a lot of time with my grandmother who lived in a nearby village and on the day of the funeral I wasn't here, I was with my grandmother in Pentrebach.

Nine year-old Bernard Thomas had a close shave in the school but managed to escape with only minor injuries. He was briefly in hospital but home by the time of the funerals.

> I didn't go, but there was a BBC team parked at the end of the street and I looked through the lens of one of the cameras. Of course the cameras were huge then. And there was a line of hearses outside the big church, people coming out of the church and the parents walking up Station Hill towards the cemetery or walking behind the convoy of hearses. That's when it all starts to sink in and that's when you start realising that it's not only old people what die. You're only just starting to come to terms with the concept of death anyway at nine or ten. Never come across anything like this before, on such a scale.

Thirteen year-old Calvin Hodkinson, whose younger brother Royston had died in the junior school, was one of the few children there.

> I wanted to go. Because I lost my brother, I wanted to be there with him.
> Oh, the funeral was massive... the streets were lined up with the older generation with their hankies, crying in the streets, seeing all these little coffins coming down the road, people walking behind. I walked behind and all, up to the cemetery... There wasn't many children up there, it was just parents.

Some people were unable to, or chose not to, go. Those who did go found it a uniquely upsetting experience. Mansel Aylward, with a young family himself, was there to see his cousin buried. But there were so many others.

There were this cohort of hearses which stretched, to my mind, ad infinitum down the streets. And I went up to the cemetery and witnessed all the cars coming through and the service that was held and that was... it brings back terrible memories because when the service was taking place and people were talking about the catastrophe, 'Why did this happen?' and speaking of God and of Providence and all this stuff, that just really upset me because I was still young and I hadn't experienced life and I thought, why do things like this happen?

Though not among the bereaved, Len Haggett was there with Fire Service colleagues.

Yes, we went to the funeral and that was, again, a traumatic experience. There's not a lot you can tell. It's something you never ever done before, nowhere you've ever been before. You've seen photographs and pictures on television and recordings of funerals and all that, but when you're dealing with that many children of that age, within sight of where it happened, it's not very pleasant. So I don't know what I can add to that.

How much more difficult then for the bereaved parents. Marilyn Brown was still in a daze of incomprehension.

By that time you really hadn't come to terms with it, you know? I don't know, we just couldn't picture anything else, we just carried on. And then of course the day of the funeral came and it was dreadful. The one thing I remember was all the people walking on the streets, obviously all dressed in black, walking along the main road going to the cemetery. It was one mass of black. And when we got there... ah, what a dreadful sight. And the funny thing, then, I couldn't cry. I just stood there. And my mother said, 'You're trying to sing!' I said, 'I'm not'. She said, 'You are, you're trying to sing'. And I was. Why was I trying to sing on a day like that? I don't know. It's so stupid afterwards, when I think about it.

Her friend Mary Morse was there to support her.

We just walked all the way up, solemn, you know, not a sound. Just footsteps. And into the cemetery and see all these... you know, you've seen it on films, but this was the reality.

Mary was there again soon after for the funeral of her friend Pat, killed with her baby and six year-old son when the tip descended on their house on Moy Road.

... and then of course a few days after I had to go again because they buried Pat up there and her two children. Because Bill was a schoolteacher and he was the only one that survived of his family there. So I went to Pat's funeral then.

It became a succession of funerals. Hettie Taylor lost count.

I don't know how many funerals we attended in the next few days because staff were buried separately but the main funeral of course was the children's and that is something... [*breaks down*] I wouldn't want to see again. The Minister came over and looked after us and one of the men from the NUT [National Union of Teachers], Glyn Llewellyn his name was, he came and watched over us. But that was something that... horrible, just horrible. Because they were buried in the same place.

*

Official responses to the disaster had started almost immediately. The Mayor of Merthyr promptly launched a disaster relief fund which very soon attracted donations from all over the world. An appeal by Princess Margaret for toys to be donated to the surviving children resulted in such an influx that storage became an acute problem. Hettie remembers seeing the initial donations.

> Oh, thousands and thousands of toys came in and they were held in the County offices. I can remember going into the room and they were floor to ceiling, of toys to give out to the children. They didn't realise how many children had gone, obviously.

The appeal had to close at the end of the month after 50,000 toys had been sent to Aberfan. Even after distribution to the children – Jeff Edwards remembers getting a toy gun – the number left over was so great that they had to be stored in a disused cinema before onward donation to other worthy causes.

Two days after the disaster a Tribunal was announced to investigate the causes of the tip slide, under the Chairmanship of Lord Justice Edmund Davies, a distinguished judge who had presided over the 1964 trial of the Great Train Robbers. An inquest into the deaths opened a day later on October 24th in the Methodist chapel. Here parents' grief and anger at what many saw as the criminal negligence of the NCB was first given vent. The *Merthyr Express* reported that as the names of the dead children were read out there were shouts of 'Murderers!' and a woman shouted out in tears, 'They have killed our children!' One father interrupted proceedings to demand that the children's death certificates should read 'Buried alive by the National Coal Board'. The *South Wales Echo* reported a moderating voice from one father: 'Today we are all leaning on each other's shoulders, lads. Let's get this over with and then we can have our say'.

The behaviour of the NCB throughout the Tribunal, and the subsequent handling of the disaster fund were to cause much more anger and anguish in the months that followed. People then did their utmost to 'have their say' – with limited effect. But for now Aberfan was still in shock. It had lost half its child population, the majority between the ages of seven and 11 – a total of 116 children. Buried or asphyxiated in the school were 52 boys and 52 girls. Six more children died in the playground of the senior school and six, including a baby, in the Moy Road houses. Of the 28 adults who died were five teachers including the Head and her Deputy, and the school meals clerk, Nansi Williams; the others were killed in their homes. The oldest victim was 78, the youngest three months.

Mercifully, 110 mostly younger children were able to escape from their classrooms dirty but unharmed. But the black glacier yielded few survivors. One of them, Gerald Tarr, in bed at his home in Moy Road when it engulfed the street, knows how lucky he is.

I don't think anybody in that row came out alive. The chap next door, Brian, he was 24. He was downstairs. Crushed to death he was. Couple of doors up there was a schoolteacher – he lost a wife and two children. He walked on that tip for days and days. He was never right after that. Never. Never got over it. Married a good few years but still young at the time. Yeah, I think all my neighbours in them houses were dead.... weren't many survivors. Only one I seen in hospital was the milkman's boy, David. His jaw was over there and his nose was over there. He was in a bit of a state when they dug him out but there was only a handful of us... How I got out of it nobody knows. It's impossible to go 50, 60 yards down the road in all that rubble and land up alive. But I died a thousand deaths, I know that.

Gerald had a miracle escape. His dog Buster wasn't so lucky.

Hardly a household was left untouched by bereavement in this close community. The local GP and the Minister of the English Baptist Church both lost a child; some men lost their whole family. Everyone knew, or was close to, at least one person who had died. Phil Thomas had gone with classmate Robert Jones on the dinner money errand that morning. Robert's body was recovered from the rubble two days later. Most of the children in Hettie's first 1965 class died with their new teacher, Michael Davies. And after 50 years, she still doesn't know if the 'lovely old man' who greeted her every morning in Moy Road on her way to school lived or died. It is likely that he was the oldest victim, 78 year-old Fred Hanson, who lived at number 79.

The work of physical recovery – to the fabric of the village and to the people – was just beginning. Its wider impact wouldn't be felt for some time.

*

Though all hope had evaporated in the days that followed the disaster, Hettie and the three other surviving teachers felt drawn to the school site.

> We kept going back. Well, it was our school, wasn't it? We felt that we just needed to be there. I think Miss Jennings was one of the last [to be found]. They wouldn't let us go to see Miss Jennings. That day she had a pink suit on and she always wore lovely jewellery, so we said, 'If it's a lady with white hair and a pink suit, then it is the Headmistress'. And they came back and they said, yes, they'd found her. Well, she would have been on her own in her office at the furthest end of the school...[*Crying*] She wouldn't have known what would have happened to the rest, I don't think...

5

AFTERMATH

On 29th October 1966 a New York photojournalist arrived in Aberfan on assignment for *Life* magazine. Chuck Rapoport had come at his own request. Like millions around the world he had heard the news and was moved to action. He found the village 'hostile ground: sad, angry, wet and cold, half of it still covered in grime from the tip's fallen slurry'. He stayed on, lodging in a pub in Aberfan Road and gradually winning the trust of local people, until Christmas Day 1966. During this time he made a series of black and white photographs.

Perhaps more than any newspaper report, these tell the story of Aberfan's grief and dislocation in the immediate aftermath of the disaster: a solitary youth heading a football in a deserted street; a mother weeping at a rain-swept graveside; bereaved parents in their homes during the long dark evenings; men in the pubs drowning unspoken sorrows. And eight year-old survivor Jeff Edwards looking up bemused at the camera from behind brimming sacks of coal, his white hair stark against the black.

Everything had changed. Nothing was ever going to be the same again. For the surviving children, who until the disaster had experienced little but a close family life, carefree play with friends and a happy, productive time in school, the change was particularly acute. It affected Jeff Edwards then and it affects him still.

My childhood ended on that day really. I had to become a different person after. I was a young kid, going to school, no cares in the world. Then the next minute I had death on my shoulder, so I had to grow up very quickly, because most of my friends perished in that disaster. There was no play after the disaster because play was frowned on within the community because so many people had lost children. Whereas before we'd kick a football about in the streets, that wasn't suitable now. Our childhood really was taken away from us. All our friends had gone and it was really hard. Really hard.

The change hit miner Gerald Tarr when he came out of hospital.

I noticed when eventually I come off the crutches, there were no kids about. The kids were playing here and playing there, but you didn't see no kids playing now. We'd lost a generation, they was all gone. And I noticed that because my wife, she was a bugger for kids like. And she said, 'All the kids is gone'. Terrible. Bad times, the whole village, a depressed feel. The village was all in mourning. It was a terrible village to live in in them days, I can tell you that now. Everyone was depressed.

Despite heroic efforts by parents to maintain a sense of normality and keep their own grief private, in homes that had lost children family life took on a sombre tone. High days and holidays were the worst, as Karen Thomas' cousin David Hopkins, whose two siblings died, recalls.

It was very hard in the beginning. Birthdays, Christmases, there was no kind of family atmosphere in the house anymore, it was like me, Mam and Dad. I appreciate now I'm older that Mam and Dad couldn't be there 100 per cent for me because they were grieving so much.

Denise Morgan couldn't help but witness the impact the death of her sister Annette had on their parents, especially their father.

> I saw a tremendous change in my father. Three weeks after [the disaster] I remember going to bed, and then they'd come up to bed and I could hear him crying, sobbing into his pillow. My mother, I'd seen her crying lots of times but not my father, I'd never ever seen my father cry or heard him cry, but I heard him constantly after that, for a long time... He just absolutely broke down and I think for a long time he became sort of lost and very emotional. I never saw him being emotional [before].

Even children who hadn't lost immediate family were affected by loss. Bernard Thomas, 10 at the time, felt the absence of familiar faces.

> ... some close friends of mine, a couple of cousins, people I knew, teachers, the Headmistress, people who were living in the houses round by the school. The Deputy Head [David Beynon], he'd just transferred from a school in Merthyr. Six foot three, a giant of a man. I remember standing next to him and looking up. I barely came up to his knee. All perished. We knew people, not just from this couple of streets, but all over the village... people you knew and all of a sudden they weren't there.

Karen Thomas, slowly recovering in hospital from serious injury, was unaware that her two cousins had died.

> I was asking about Angela and Stephen. There was no response. They didn't tell me anything till the day before the funeral... when they told me that Angela and Stephen had died and they were coming up for the funerals. I just broke down then. I was uncontrollable. I wanted to come home then but they said I couldn't leave the hospital... I

was just lost then, after I lost Angela. [*crying*] We were so close. We were always together and life wasn't the same without her. There was only a month between us and we were like sisters. And I still think about her today.

Phil Thomas was in a critical condition in hospital for some time before his distraught elder brother Alan, 12, had news of him. Now he understands his parents' reticence.

I didn't know for a long time where he was, because my mother and father didn't know whether Phil was going to pull through. I think they didn't want to build my hopes up, give me a false security. That's how protective [my mother] could be. She wouldn't build me up and the next minute: 'You've lost Philip'. She would tell me if we'd lost Philip, but no in-between.

I was taken to my Auntie's, myself and my sister Ann, and we spent nearly three weeks there. The thing is, the not knowing, just seeing your parents in the evening after visiting hours in the hospitals... In those three weeks I was out of Aberfan there was a lot, not that I missed out on, but a lot went on, the clearing up. There was no school or anything, you couldn't go to school. It wasn't the place to be because there was no happiness there anymore. And my parents had put me in the care of my Auntie for protection, for the love and attention that was needed.

But I still didn't know about Philip and I started asking questions. I became a child that wanted to know. I was up there at my Auntie's and all the children had been buried. I had not seen any of that. I was kept out of it. The only thing I ever seen was photographs, that's all I ever seen of the funerals in Aberfan.

They told me about a week or two later that he was alive and in hospital. They came after visiting and told me that he was stable, he's in hospital and he's OK. And that was enough. That was it. That was enough for me then.

And that's why I had a strop with my Auntie then, because I wanted to go home. I knew he was alright. I threw a tantrum. I wanted to go home. And I chastised my Auntie, [*crying*] for at least three days I wouldn't talk to her and she'd never ever let me forget that, right up until the day she died. She'd say, 'You can throw a real wobbly when you want to'.

But getting home and being home, things were different. There was that emptiness. We lived in the same bedroom. His bed was opposite my bed. His wall was plastered with photographs of footballers and my wall was plastered with fish because I liked fishing.

*

Feelings of anxiety and guilt were common among surviving children like Jeff Edwards.

We experienced something that would shatter our lives, change our lives completely and we would become totally different people. We suffered from guilt because we had survived and others hadn't. We had to come to terms with our guilt, and it's very difficult, even to this day to say, well, why did you survive and someone next door didn't?

Like all the surviving children, Bernard Thomas

... grew up facing the parents and siblings and relatives of the ones who died. It wasn't easy because for a long time after, Aberfan was a very, very sad village.

The only surviving sibling of three, David Hopkins has borne a particular burden over the years. It was only by chance that his mother stopped him escorting his brother and sister to school that morning, because she had the day off and wanted to spend precious time with him.

It was very difficult to be the survivor of that kind of thing. Not so much then, but in the later years, you just feel you should have been there with them. You just feel, it should have been me as well, not just them, it should have happened to me.

Though what has since been recognised as 'survivor guilt' took time – perhaps years – to come to the surface for some people, for many of the children other symptoms appeared soon after the disaster and continued into adolescence and beyond. Being starved of air left Jeff with epilepsy after the disaster, but the memory of being buried with a dead classmate beside him had an even greater impact. He now understands that he was suffering from PTSD.

Whilst I had head and stomach injuries, it was the psychological problems that would go on. I would have nightmares, bed-wetting, irritability, unable to concentrate. All these are classic symptoms of post-traumatic stress disorder. We now know what it is. In those days it didn't exist. It would take years and years to get over that and the nightmares of that girl on my shoulder and the sense of being involved in it would not go away. I still have those nightmares on occasions.

Jeff's mother, Tessie, confirms the many sleepless nights:

His nerves were terrible. I mean, in the middle of the night he'd be crying and screaming, and my husband then, he'd say, 'No, you stay there, I'll go'. And he'd go in the bed and lie with him until he went to sleep. But we had that for a very long time.

Like Jeff, Bernard Thomas suffered more from the psychological effects in the coming months and years.

Not so much physically, couple of cuts, a bit of bruising.
Walking wounded, you might say. But mentally, for years,
it's been a different kettle of fish. I was only nine at the
time and I don't suppose the full impact really sunk in. I
didn't know at the time how close I was to actually being
killed. Within a hair's breadth, an inch of my life. It
affected me for a number of years after in my teens, and
in my 20s and 30s... I did quite a bit of crying privately,
couldn't sleep. I couldn't hear tip lorries rumbling on
the road outside without rushing into the living room
thinking the tip was coming down again. Loss of concentration at school. Drinking too much to camouflage it,
blank it all out, for comfort.

For the adults too, the impact affected behaviour. After losing
her daughter Janette, Marilyn Brown was over-protective
with her son Robert.

After that I always wanted to know, what's he doing?
Where's he going? I didn't want him to go anywhere, but
of course he was young, he didn't understand what was
going on.

Hettie Taylor was aware that her own parents had become
unusually protective.

When I was at home, I felt I was being watched all the
time. You know, was I going to have a breakdown or
something?

She didn't have a breakdown but some effects were immediate
and some have stayed with her.

I can't say I've had flashbacks. Some noises upset me. And
the same with the children. When we were at the school
in Mount Pleasant there was a tree and when a certain

wind would come there would be a tapping against the window. I looked at the children and the children looked at me and we were both frightened. Certain things triggered us all off. So we went out into the yard together. We were frightened of certain noises.

The disaster affected her colleague Howell Williams badly. He aspired to be a Head Teacher but this wasn't to be. After leaving the new Ynysowen primary school he moved out of the village and taught in schools in Merthyr. Eventually he had a breakdown and left teaching in 1990, his ambition unfulfilled.

Even people not directly affected found that the experience of being at the scene had a later impact on their behaviour. Salvation Army volunteer Dorothy Burns soon discovered that

... I couldn't stay in the house with any doors shut. All my doors had to be open, for a long, long time. The feeling of being shut in was dreadful, absolutely awful.

Mansel Aylward was a young medical student who had volunteered checking casualties, shifting rubble and comforting the bereaved.

There was no such thing as Post Traumatic Stress Disorder in those days and indeed I didn't realise for about 20 years or so after Aberfan that I had got that, because I used to have recurring dreams, I used to wake up in a sweat remembering instances, in particular that one where we found that classroom with the teacher and children. I realised that it had affected me, but I thought that would be normal – you know, it would be abnormal if I didn't feel like that. But now, as we know, there is a condition, PTSD.

Gerald Tarr's post-disaster claustrophobia affected his work prospects.

I got over the nightmares. 'Course, it's still cut in my memory like. I was claustrophobic for a long time after that. It's done something to my mind – done something to my peanut brain, I couldn't get closed in, you know? 'Course you don't realise you're claustrophobic. They sent me down to Talygarn [Miners'] Hospital and I had this treatment for a couple of weeks and they retrain you, like, to get your head together, they take you into a false mine. It looks exactly like you're underground. Painted coal and all the rest of it. I went in there with all the boys, and all of a sudden I got up and run out of there. I just flew. He seen me afterwards. He said, 'You'll be no good for underground'. I said, 'Why? If I give up, I lose my job'. 'Claustrophobic', he said, 'you'll feel like that for a long time. Don't go back underground'.

I never went back, never went back to the pit after. They put me on top of the pit. Couldn't stick it. There was more dust than there was underground! And the noise was terrible! Things churning and... couldn't stick it. I started on a building site shortly after that, pipe-laying down Dowlais.

For some of the children too, there were profound after-effects. Phil Thomas had been critically injured.

Where shall we start? I had a bad head injury. I had epileptic fits through it, which I don't have now. I lost my three fingers on my right hand. My ear was hanging off – they put it back on. Scars across my face, both elbows. I had a spleen removed, fractured pelvis, which they said I would never walk again. But I did thank God. Both knees cut badly, I got a hole on the inside of my leg here. Stitches, hundreds of stitches.

Because of the blow on my head, the damage, I had memory loss. They used to keep track on me from the hospital as I got older and I can't remember nothing from the day I was born till I was 10. People say, 'Do you miss your fingers?' Well, I can't remember having fingers, so losing them... So if someone said I was born without fingers then I'd say, fair enough.

*

The treatment of people who'd suffered major trauma where death is close at hand was under-developed in 1966. What little was known came from the experience of 'shell-shocked' soldiers after the First World War and the impact of military conflict on men's minds. Aberfan was something new and terrible in peacetime Britain – a disaster involving whole families and large numbers of young children. There were no immediate tools to help people cope with the after-effects, or even a proper understanding of what these effects were likely to be or how long they might last.

The pioneering Tavistock Institute in London, perhaps one of the best equipped at the time to lend aid, offered advice and support to Merthyr Council. It proposed sending a team to Aberfan and this would form the basis for an important and potentially useful research study for the future.

In a proud close-knit community where particular value was placed on quiet fortitude and self-reliance, and where a residual fear of 'the men in white coats' and psychiatric medicine meant swift removal to 'the loony bin', these were politely declined. The people of Aberfan, having suffered so much, were not to be used as guinea-pigs; they would cope themselves, in their own way.

In fact a rudimentary form of counselling was offered to school-age children by the local education authority's child psychiatrist and psychological assessments were attempted in order to contribute to compensation claims. A few children also benefited from sessions with a psychiatrist at the local mental hospital but Jeff Edwards was not one of them.

The psychiatric services that were there were very much in their infancy. They tried to help but their value to us was not that good if I'm honest. They were trying their very, very best and I always remember one particular psychiatrist and they told you, well, when you have these bad feelings about what you saw, think of nice things, like your birthday party. But when I think of birthday parties post-disaster, all my friends had died, so there was nothing to think about really, other than the loss of those children who would have been there.

It was up to the people themselves whether they took up these services, where offered. Many, like Marilyn Brown, preferred to keep things within their own circle.

People came to find out if we needed help, you know, did we want someone to talk to? From quite a few sources, but we refused their help because we said, we have good family, good friends, and we know we can rely on them all. And we did. We did rely on them all. And they helped us a great deal.

Her friend Mary Morse was another who felt that help was best given in the home.

Counselling came to the village then. But we counselled our own children. I counselled my daughter and my husband and I did it in our own home. She didn't want to go and see a psychiatrist; I wouldn't have put her through that at five. We talked it over and we came through it, but I still live that day every day of the week and year. Never forget it. I can remember everything.

If you look back, perhaps we all should have been to the psychiatrist [*laughs*] but I mean, you know, if you've got a good family and a good family life, you've no need to go anywhere. You don't need outside assistance. You just need friends. A friend can do more than anything. Sometimes friends can be better than family. You can choose your friends but you can't choose your family! But I'm lucky, I've got both.

Phil Thomas was still receiving treatment for his injured hand where he lost three fingers. He recalls having to see 'a teacher' in Merthyr. Whether he was there for tuition to ease him back into schooling, or whether he was being assessed by an educational psychologist isn't clear. Either way, the sessions don't appear to have been very rigorous, unlike his hospital treatment:

> Before I went back to school I used to go three times a week, a Monday a Wednesday and a Friday I had to go to St Tydfil's for wax treatment. They used to dip your hand in the wax, wrap it in a towel, wait 15-20 minutes and then they would work the finger, massage to get it to work like. And I used to go up to the Further Education building, top of town in Merthyr and a teacher, a Mr Smith I think it was, I used to go into his room and he was a very nice gentleman. He always used to be there with his feet up on his desk and his pipe in his mouth and he used to say, 'Come and do some reading by 'ere, fella'. And we'd have the books out. I'd say, 'I'd rather be making an aeroplane out'a balsawood', and he'd say, 'Go on then!'

For the rescue services there was no at-work counselling. The men dealt with it in their own way. Part-time fireman Allan Lewis who'd found the bodies of four small girls and their teacher, talked to the rest of his crew on the way back from the disaster.

> It didn't sink in straight away. But when I got back to the transport home, all of the other boys were still in their clean tunics where I looked as if I just been in a

mud-wrestling competition. And they wanted to know exactly what happened and I did tell them. So that was a little bit of relief, rather than it building up inside, talking to them on the way home. No counselling whatever, but that was about the only counselling I had, really, was to them, because there was no-one here, where I was working, so I just told them and that was it.

It was upsetting... I think I did block it out of my mind. Because I'd been in the Fire Service and I had to see other bodies, like, in fire and different things, so you got to put it out of your mind. It was part of the job, you had to go out again. But yes, I did try and blank it out. Hard, because every now and again it'd come on television and bring the memory back. Whenever you'd see it on television it all fetched it back. I had many sleepless nights about it, picturing those little girls and the teacher and everything. It was a very, very sad time. But I survived.

Fireman Len Haggett remembers:

I can only talk about it from my personal angle of it. Within the Fire Service that was the type of thing you had to do if you were involved in house fires where there were fatalities or rescues, or road traffic accidents. You dealt with it. Again, with children it was always more traumatic and firemen would talk about it in those instances, you know, you would discuss it. But the Aberfan disaster was something different because the number of children and people who had died within such a small space and in areas you would have thought would have been safe. And you were looking at, in some aspects, at what could have been a war zone.

So I don't know what was around or what was available. I don't know whether the children had counselling. At the Fire Service counselling wasn't there then, you got on with the job you had to do and you got over any

inhibitions you had, talking about it or going away somewhere quietly on your own and giving vent to your
feelings.

From a personal point of view, had counselling been
available at that time, I don't think I would have discussed
it. I think I would have done what I done - just try to force
it out of my memory and live with it and not try to think
too deeply about it or too often. And to obliterate – if you
can obliterate – some of the scenes that were there that
day. So I don't know that counselling would have been
any advantage to me. But then I'm talking in hindsight. I
don't know.

Like Len, the men tended to try and put the whole thing out of
their minds and carry on as normally as possible. Rescue
workers might talk about what had happened among themselves
– but rarely the horror of what they'd seen and experienced. For
Mines Rescue worker Bob Griffiths

> ...it was at least three or four days before any of us got
> together in the tea room or something like that, and we'd
> talk about it then, talk about our experience of the incident,
> but we talked about it in – how can I put this without
> sounding hard or anything like that? We'd talk about it in
> a jokingly sort of way, and little things that happened that
> made you laugh and things like that, even in adversity, and
> those are the type of things, and we'd talk about it in that
> way… and I suppose that's the way we actually coped.

Even so, memories of the trauma would re-emerge.

> [Months later] very often I'd wake up in the night, cold
> sweat, thinking about the children and physically crying,
> but time heals to a certain extent, and as it went on longer
> and longer, the dreams disappear. It did surprise me that
> I would wake up thinking about it and dreaming about it,

because I thought I had put it in a compartment, in my memory bank and that was it. But obviously certain things would trigger it, and there's nothing you can do about that, that's what you've got a memory for.

*

'Putting it in a compartment' and 'being strong' seemed to be the way most people tried to deal with what had happened. Apart from the funerals, there was little opportunity – offered or taken – for communal grief. Grieving was confined to homes, families, perhaps with very close friends. As Marilyn Brown recalls, open displays of grief, mentioning the disaster or acknowledging another's grief was too difficult.

I think you couldn't cry, because a lot of people were in the same position as yourself and you were afraid to let yourself down, because when you were with people in the same position you tried to keep yourself... light, and not get emotional about it.

I remember one instance when we were passing one another in the street and I hadn't seen this lady for a while, and we just looked at one another. She'd lost her little girl. Not saying anything, just looked at one another, and said, 'Hello, how are you? OK?' and carried on. And that's how it seemed. It seemed you'd keep... and not show your emotions, you know? Because you knew that they were in the same position as yourself and you couldn't let yourself down. But I couldn't cry for a long, long time after that. I couldn't let myself do it.

I could never sort of open up. I don't think I've ever cried in front of anybody, not that I can recall... You could talk about it to your husband and I would talk about it to my immediate friends, and I would talk about it to my family because my mother would say, 'Well, you've got to talk about it, get it out of your system, you know, feel that bit of relief'. And I'd say, 'No, I can't see that'. No, you felt you wanted to keep it in because it was helping you then to think everything was OK. But it wasn't. It wasn't OK.

Jeff Edwards' mother Tessie cried out of sight of Jeff and his sister.

You've got to be strong. It's very difficult, I'd have my crying upstairs, or downstairs if they weren't there. My nerves went to pieces, but you had to be strong, for both of the children.

Gloria Davies lost a much-loved cousin, Brian Harris, who lived next door to Gerald Tarr at 84 Moy Road.

I can't say enough about him, because everyone liked him, and he dressed lovely, he always had lovely nice collars on and a suit, and he was something special. He was a very special person to me, and he was such a clean person, and then he died in that terrible blackness, I couldn't believe it.

When I did go back to work, I had to try to be strong, but people realised that if I went in the corner to cry, they didn't mind, because they realised that everyone was so upset… and you just had to find strength from somewhere, but we got through it.

Child survivor Karen Thomas had also lost her cousins Angela and Stephen with whom she'd had an almost sibling-close relationship, but there was no discussion of the disaster at home.

As a family we never spoke about anything. My mother tried to keep us strong and, you know, it's like a matter of fact, it happened, it's something you'll never forget but your life has got to go on.

*

Apart from family networks, other forms of support were to hand. With help from the Tavistock, the local authority appointed Audrey Davey, a family caseworker, in November. She stayed on in Aberfan for two years, visiting bereaved families, listening if they wanted to talk and encouraging them to set up their own informal support groups.

Local churches also lent support – to their congregations and to the wider community. Though church and chapel were less influential in the valleys by the mid-1960s than they had once been and regular attendance had fallen off sharply, there were still six places of worship in the village and more in nearby Merthyr Vale. Their leaders played a significant role in bringing the community through its initial mourning into slow recovery despite examples of individual loss: the Rev Kenneth Hayes, minister of the Zion English Baptist chapel had lost a son himself.

The disaster had momentarily shaken religious faith for people like Hettie Taylor.

> I was a chapel-goer. My mother and I went to Welsh Baptist. Yes, I did have a strong faith. And I think my first reaction after Aberfan was, well, you know, if there is a God, why did He let this happen? To school-children. But then, it was man's foolishness really, wasn't it? Not God. I don't know, I think it shook my faith. I still believe, but I'm not a practising Christian at the moment and haven't been for a while. But I think there must be something greater, otherwise perhaps all of us would have gone. Some of us survived. But yes, it did shake my faith.

Jeff Edwards recalls that

> ... some people turned against religion completely. You know, if there is a God, why did it happen? I was brought up in a pretty religious family. My mother always attended church; it was a very important part of her life. Me and

my sister were always brought up in that ethic of churchgoing. And obviously I wondered if there was a God after that. One of the gravestones up in the memorial says 'Suffer the little children to come unto me'. And that sums it up in terms of what happened. The children suffered. And they all went to God. But I still am religious and go to church on occasion. But I don't criticise people who've abandoned their faith because of what happened... parents don't expect to lose their children before their own demise. It's a huge loss, a huge thing to come to terms with and many parents haven't come to terms with that, and probably they never will. That's why people in the community will never be the same again. They've become different people.

Those with strongly-held religious convictions like Salvationist Dorothy Burns were certainly challenged by the experience.

I found it very difficult. I thought I would have lost my faith when I saw that, but I didn't, it made me stronger. Because of my faith and my belief I was OK, I carried on.

June Vaughan was a lay preacher and Sunday School teacher.

I didn't cry until the Sunday when the Sunday paper came and it had photographs of some of the children and of course I knew them all and I cried then to see so many of them so soon after it had happened. You felt, all these children, is it possible? We lost 17 children from the Sunday School and they were very, very close to us. You knew the parents and you knew the grandparents. They weren't strangers' children, they were friends' children.

I think it must have tested everybody's faith. Why on Friday when it was half term the following week, why did it happen? This is the question that must have shaken people's faith to the core. Why it couldn't have been the next week. People would have died but not to the extent... not all those children.

I would not be worshipping a God if I thought He had allowed this to happen. There would be no way I could reconcile myself to the idea that 'why didn't it happen the next week?' But I wasn't bereaved, so I wasn't in the situation...

No-one questioned me regarding my faith. I think for one thing, they realised the disaster was man-made. Also I think they had enough on their minds to occupy their time and thoughts with living day-to-day, coping with this dreadful tragedy that had happened to them.

June offered what help she felt she could when she went into people's homes.

You waited for them to speak if they wanted to speak. By meeting them and speaking to them, it was all you felt you could do. I certainly didn't want to go out giving any words of advice to them. If you've not been through a similar tragedy, you don't understand really how people are feeling, so it's not until you lose someone very close to you that you begin to understand.

Her minister, the Reverend Irving Penberthy, was one of those who inspired the first efforts at rebuilding community spirit. Together with June and founder members Marilyn Brown, Mary Morse and others, they established a new group in the village. The Young Wives – later just 'the Wives' – were to have a transformative role in helping the women of Aberfan look to a more positive future.

*

Aberfan's primary school had been destroyed (the remains were finally demolished the following April, together with the undamaged senior school) but its surviving children still needed to be educated. Many children, like Jeff Edwards, were hesitant to go back to school.

> We couldn't go to school for a long time. I was afraid to go to school because I was afraid the tip was going to come down again. Schools meant danger to us.

Parents were reluctant too. But the local education authority had its responsibilities and teacher Hettie Taylor still had a job to do.

> They wanted the children to come back. It was time for us to come together and start again in some sort of a school situation. So we went around the houses talking to the children, for them to know that we were OK and everything and they wondered how we were going to start the school again.
>
> We started all together, infants and juniors in the Gordon Lennox Club and they gave us the upstairs room. The Director [of Education] came and he said, we're going to see if we can get the children back to school, they needed to come back together. They wondered then how many children they would get because of lot of parents said they'd go to somewhere else. That's understandable. Then one or two would come, then a few more would come, and it was surprising how many children did come back. Obviously the ones that had been injured took longer to come back. But that was a good time, when they were coming [back]. We weren't teaching, we were doing games and puzzles and colouring and things like that, but they were coming back, they were seeing their friends, they were seeing us and they were all talking to one another. And I think that's what helped us really, to be as normal as we were, because we just carried on. We were their teachers and the children were wonderful.

For the infants, there was another Infants School in Aberfan. There was room there for Mair and Rene's classes to go. So then that left Howell and myself then with what was left of the Junior School. Obviously we couldn't have a school building. So they put caravans down on the park site so Howell and I had these two caravans and Howell was the boss man, you know, he was the Head. So we went round telling the children that we had these caravans down there and trying to persuade them to come. Most of the children were ready to come. Some of the parents weren't ready to let them go, but they started to come to the school. To let their children out of their sight and let them come back to school again must have been hard for them.

We had like one long caravan. Howell was one end and I was the other end and there was somewhere they could play so we could have playtimes. Over a few weeks I think, children started coming back to the park. In the end, we had all the children back.

Bringing the children back to school was, for her, the only positive response to the negative feelings this terrible event had brought out.

It was anger, to think that this tip could take the lives of so many children [*crying*]. To think that you had survived. Why me? Why was my class the last one to take it? The only thing you could do then was to do as much as you could for the ones that survived. Those children had lost their friends, they'd lost their teachers, so you had to be there. And that's how I think we all felt. That they needed – as much as we needed – to be with those children.

The school was going to go on and we were going to make it work. The aim was to make that school as good as it had been, and to remember the people who had worked there. They were such wonderful people. So, for us, it was to continue that with the children, and to make sure that those children were happy. They were in the same school, in a different place, but it was still Pantglas School.

We needed them as well. We were offered I think it was a couple of weeks later – if there was a position – at any school in the County. We could go to another school. But none of us wanted to. Because that was our school. We needed to see their faces as much as they needed to see ours. The children left behind, they needed to see us and know that their school was going to go on. We were going to beat this. We were going to go on.

I think that's what drove us. We wanted those children to have what they would have had if the school had stayed.

This, Hettie believes, was the start of her own rehabilitation as well as that of the children.

When I was with the children, the children were looking at me in a different way, they were making me feel special and I suppose that's where the bond comes because we'd been through everything together. Being with the children helped us; we needed to see one another. They were coming back to as they'd been before, and so were we. They were the only ones that could help us and maybe they felt that we were the only ones that could help them because being with people outside of that situation, it doesn't matter how much sympathy they had for us, it wasn't the same as we had for one another. In a way I suppose it was therapeutic.

*

Things were starting to look up too for 12 year-old Alan Thomas. At last Phil was sufficiently recovered to receive visitors. The brothers could finally be reunited after weeks of pain and anguish.

I think it was either six or eight weeks before I seen him and when I did see him it was in hospital in Cardiff. We walked long corridors and we got to the ward, Philip was sat up in bed and the big old crepe bandages all round his head like a turban.

And upon meeting him, the first words he said to me was, 'I've lost my fingers! Look, I've got a boxing glove!' And he laughed. I said, 'That's alright, that's not a problem.' And we wrapped arms round each other and basically cried. And that was it, the warmth of his body, and the smell of antiseptic. We were right then, everything was right. Didn't have a care in the world. My brother was happy, my sister was giggling. And it became routine then, didn't miss a visit, whether he was in a bad mood or not – because he was up and down for a long time. We were reunited. [*Emotional*] And we're still the same today.

Things that went on in the village, quietly they moved on... There was no school. I was always up in the woods but every day was visiting time in Cardiff. The Round Table sent a driver and a car down. Personal, individual people gave up their time and took my parents and myself down to see Philip. My sister would sometimes come and sometimes we would leave her with my grandmother and other family in Aberfan. But it went on for months and months and months. He was very badly damaged... He's got the biggest caterpillar I've ever seen on his belly [*emotional*] – it must be about 12 inches long – where they removed his spleen and stitched him back up. Very lucky boy. They said he'd never walk again. He managed to father four children, so he proved them wrong!

*

By November 24th, a little over a month after the disaster, the Aberfan relief fund had reached the unprecedented sum of £1m after money had been donated – in large sums and small – from all over the world. Its charitable objects, established after some delay, were: *'For the relief of all persons who have suffered... and are thereby in need; and for any charitable purpose for the benefit of inhabitants of Aberfan on 21 October 1966'.*

By the end of the year the fund had already paid out nearly £25,000 for immediate relief and a payment of £50 to bereaved families at Christmas. Debates about who should be represented on the fund committee, and on what and whom the money should be spent were seized on – and often characterised as rows - by the press. Media intrusion was a problem in the first year and on subsequent anniversaries. When the village wanted to be left alone to cope as it thought fit, newspaper reporters were often on hand intent on finding the most sensational or heart-rending stories. There was a feeling that positive stories were being ignored at a time when Aberfan – and Wales – needed them. People unused to dealing with the press felt they were being manipulated, as Mary Davies recalls.

> The journalist from one of the newspapers came to my door, asking if he could interview me, and I said well, I'll talk to you, but he was putting words into my mouth so I said I think we better end this conversation. We aren't getting anywhere.

But there were some positive stories and parents, seduced perhaps by the novelty of the television cameras, allowed their children to be filmed. Jeff Edwards remembers giving an interview – the first of his life – for the Canadian Broadcasting Corporation.

> I was playing with my Hornby trainset, all laid out on a big board and there was this Canadian Pacific train, which they thought was fantastic because it was good publicity for Canada... and they gave me a red Raleigh bike as my gift, the latest model with a seat on the back.

We used to go everywhere on bikes then. I was very proud
of this red bike.

*

There was certainly anger and emotion in the village, most of it
directed at the National Coal Board whose Chairman, Lord
Robens, from his earliest interview had denied knowledge of
any natural springs under tip No 7. And the NCB's case at the
Tribunal Inquiry, which began on 29th November 1966, was
aggressively defensive, maintaining that the disaster was
essentially unforeseeable.

Everyone in Aberfan knew this was untrue: the springs were
marked on Ordnance Survey maps but tipping had continued,
regardless of two earlier slides. There had been previous flooding, and residents' complaints and petitions against the tips had
been ignored. The Head Teacher of Pantglas, Miss Jennings,
had herself alerted the local education authority of the danger
to her school posed by tip No. 7. All the warning signs were
there. It was a disaster waiting to happen.

Facing up to its responsibilities on the ground, the NCB did
provide some immediate relief, supplying 37 caravans for the
homeless displaced from Moy Road – though it later attempted
to charge rent for these. Compensation paid for the loss of the
children was finally agreed in principle between bereaved
parents and the Coal Board the following May. Parents received
£500 per child, in addition to an initial payment of £50 made
soon after the event. The loss of working adults was valued
more highly, the adult injured likewise: Gerald Tarr received
£5000. Hettie, her fellow teachers and the surviving children all
received £200. Trauma and its after-effects, little understood,
were largely ignored in the compensation calculations.

We had £200, the same as the children. We didn't want
that, we didn't want anything to be honest. If they think
that children's lives were worth £200... It's appalling,
really appalling.

No amount of money could compensate for a lost child, wife or husband. For Mary Morse the money was irrelevant.

> The thing is, a lot of money came into the village, people appreciated it but it meant nothing to us because we had more than money could ever buy. I had my daughter.

*

The Tribunal report, published in August of the following year, entirely vindicated the village and those who had warned about the dangerous condition of the tip. The Coal Board, it found, was irrefutably responsible for the tragedy, but not through wilful negligence as many in Aberfan believed, but because of 'bungling ineptitude' and weak leadership. Some, including perhaps Lord Justice Davies himself, expected legal action against the NCB or its employees to follow as a consequence of his report, or at the very least resignations and rolling heads. But there was no action against any individual or body corporate and neither Robens nor any NCB manager or worker lost their job.

This still rankles with some survivors; the anger is still there. For others any bitterness has long since passed. Regardless of how they felt about the apportionment of blame and the impact of subsequent betrayals by the authorities, they all had to face the following years with the mixed legacy left by the Aberfan disaster. Could good come out of it? How would they respond to the challenges ahead, and what could be made of the lives so fundamentally altered by the tragedy?

Bernard Thomas

Bob Griffiths

David Hopkins

Denise Morgan

Calvin Hodkinson

Jeff Edwards

Tessie Edwards

Len Haggett

Dave Thomas

Dorothy Burns

Sheila Davies

Malcolm Davies

Roy Hamer

Mary Davies

Mary Morse

Phil and Alan Thomas, still close.

Phil reunited with Len Haggett and Dave Thomas after 50 years.

Hettie Taylor

Karen Thomas

Marilyn Brown

June Vaughan

Gerald Tarr

6

LEGACY

The years that followed the disaster were the most difficult the village had yet faced. As one elderly resident recalled:

> [The community of Aberfan] was vacant somehow. We tried, but it took a long time for things to happen, to come back to normal. Well, you don't go back to normal, I mean there's a place missing in the houses that lost children.

Not only were grief and memory still fresh and the streets empty of children, the people had to live for some time with the evidence of the tragedy still all too apparent around them. It took six months and a deputation to Merthyr Council before the ruins of Pantglas School started to be cleared. And the cause of their troubles was still looming over them. Though work had started on topping out tip No. 7 by the end of 1966, it was more than two years before it was removed altogether, and then not without bitter controversy.

In the meantime and for many years after, tipping from Merthyr Vale colliery continued, and so did the dirt and flooding invading its streets. Gerald Tarr, largely recovered from his injuries and living elsewhere in Aberfan after his house in Moy Road was destroyed, suffered two major floods caused by tipping on Council land close to his new home.

> It was one disaster after another one, I couldn't see the bloody end. And of course the wife had to go through it

an' all. All my photographs went out in the flood. We were all wiped out. I wish to God I'd never come here. I mean I don't mind the place, I don't mind the people. I don't mind the village, they're alright. It's just what happened to me, one thing after another like.

Those affected by the floods took legal action against the NCB and Merthyr Council which ended in victory in the High Court but no compensation was awarded. Coming on top of the disaster, this left Gerald with a legacy of bitterness against the NCB.

I had happy days before it happened. And years of sad things after it happened. I tell you, the NCB for flooding me out twice for dumping outside my house. Found guilty, but no compensation. They didn't pay the penalty for that. They got away with everything. That made me mad.

There were many reasons for the already suffering community of Aberfan to feel let down by authority. The Tribunal had found the National Coal Board unequivocally culpable for the disaster yet no-one had been brought to account in a court of law. Now residents had to summon the strength to mount a campaign for the removal of the seven tips still surrounding them, responsibility for which the NCB seemed reluctant to accept. The Treasury similarly refused to pick up the tab.

The scandalous solution to the cost of removing the tips was to raid the disaster fund for a contribution of £150,000 – 10% of the fund's value and worth about £3million in today's money. Though this surely stretched the letter and spirit of its charitable objects to the limit and beyond, the fund's trustees felt pressured to agree. The Charity Commission did not intervene and Labour Prime Minister Harold Wilson was uneasy but gave his approval. Only the longstanding local MP, S O Davies, resigned in disgust from the trustees, saying it was 'the meanest thing I've seen in 34 years in Parliament'.

Despite the findings of the Tribunal Inquiry, it looked to many as if the Coal Board under Lord Robens was doing its best to limit its financial liability for the disaster. Compensation payments, agreed in principle in May 1967, were not paid out until three years later in 1970, the fund having to bear the burden of relief payments to families in the interim. This was problematic: it took a while for the legal status of the fund – set up in necessary haste – to be clarified and even then unnecessary pain was caused by the Charity Commission's insistence at one point that money could only be paid to parents where it could be established they had been 'close' to their child or children. In such a tight-knit family-oriented community this heaped insult on injury.

The Aberfan Disaster Appeal finally closed at £1,606,929 on January 31st 1967 after nearly 90,000 individual donations had been received from the widest possible sections of society: from widowed pensioners from their savings to children giving up their pocket money. One of the largest single donations was a handsome £100 given at a gala dinner organised by the Cardiff Committee for Aid to Aberfan by the notorious gangsters Ronnie and Reggie Kray, later jailed for life for murder. At the time this was revealed in 2010, Jeff Edwards told the *South Wales Echo* that their gift showed how widely the impact of the disaster had been felt.

With such an unprecedentedly large fund at their disposal it was inevitable that there should be passionate debate about how and where the money should be spent. What proportion of the money should be sunk in 'bricks and mortar' and what given direct to individuals? How much to memorialise the dead and how much to sustain the living? Decisions were for the 15 trustees to make but even after local protests only a third of them directly represented the people and interests of Aberfan. The appointment of a Secretary-Treasurer at an annual salary of £3000 plus car allowance also raised eyebrows. Exaggerated press reports of a community riven by rows about money helped keep other, deeper, wounds open.

Even as a teenager, Alan Thomas saw the impact on friends and neighbours.

A lot of people, bitter, angry, as I grew up. Anxiety, desperation, some people. Drink, other people. There's been suicides. It's something that should never have happened. I believe the time the tipping was going on, they knew about it. They knew it would move. Lot of politics, not a lot of support given to us, in fact they made the Aberfan fund pay for the removal of the tips. Aberfan before the disaster, it was a little haven... the summers we used to have... it's a beautiful place. But that disaster changed everything, changed the people.

If the adults were changed, so were the surviving children. Jeff Edwards' physical injuries had healed but the symptoms of his continuing distress were still evident.

I hated crowds, I couldn't go anywhere where there were crowds. I couldn't sleep, I lacked concentration, I was wetting the bed. These were huge things that our parents had to deal with. We all suffered the same symptoms. One of the difficult things was getting back to normality – if there was a normality.

Phil Thomas had suffered life-threatening injuries: as well as internal injuries he lost three fingers and his ear was almost torn off. But he was a fighter.

As for my fractured pelvis, I always remember the first day they got me out of bed and I hadn't stood for... it might have been the beginning of December, and they said, right, stand up. And they stood me up by the side of the bed and I thought, oh, this is good. Then I went all giddy and fell flat on my face. And as I was just about to go, they caught me and they said, 'Take your time now, sit up'. Well I think my Mam and Dad was due down, I think it was five o'clock Visiting. And I'd spent all day with two stools across the hospital ward floor. Stool. Step. Stool. Step. And by the time my mother come, I walked out of the ward to meet her. [*Upset*] Yes, that was very important to me.

He bore his tortuously slow recovery with stoicism.

A Dr Treasure done a lot of work on my legs. When they transferred me down to Prince of Wales a Dr Miric Williams done my hand... I used to go then in January, to Chepstow. Used to be the skin graft and burns unit. They always used to cut a piece off my leg, do the skin graft on my face. Yeah, my ear [sewn back on] never bothered me, it's only that I had so much wrong with me at once, that I think I just got on with it. Never moaned about it.

Once he was back home with his parents and brother Alan, his mother had her own way of dealing with his ongoing recovery.

When I came home, there were a few ground rules. Never mentioned in my house. Never spoke about. I'm not sure how many there were in my class – some say 32, some say 37. They were big classes. Only three of us come out that day. It was kept from me. I didn't know all the time I was in hospital. My Mum was a very good woman in the sense that she protected us as a family, so when I come home from hospital the house never changed. We got on with everything, everyday life. Sat down for evening meals, never spoke about it. We always went on holidays. Porthcawl. Every Whitsun, every fortnight Miners' Shutdown, Porthcawl. Loved it. Loved it... We led a normal life. Never spoke about the disaster, never spoke about my injuries, but she looked after us.

I wasn't allowed to go near the cemetery. Or where they were taking the tip away. I think I was wrapped up so well by my Mam that the extent of the disaster she kept from me. My Mam was great. My Dad was great as well but my Mam was Number One in the house, she was the boss, like. She done a marvellous job of protecting us after the disaster. It put years on my mother and her nerves went. She become a bit of a recluse, she never used to go out anywhere, she used to stay in the house, didn't like to go out with people.

I suppose at the time, '66, there was no counselling. I never went for any therapy for what happened. Mam looked after us, never spoke about it, I had all my hospital appointments, I was quite busy after, going three times a week to St Tydfil's, then to the Education. Never used to speak about it, never ever. And that most probably was my Mam's way of dealing with it. And I think that it worked, because over the years I never dwelled on it, I never looked back. Mam just protected us. No press, no newspaper pestering me. My mother said, 'No, leave him alone'. And that's how it was.

Alan agrees that their mother was determined to give them a sense of normality but she protected them fiercely too: the family drew in on itself.

She made sure we had a holiday twice a year. One of my father's workmates bought a caravan in Porthcawl and for years we went to Porthcawl and then to West Wales in this caravan... we had some fabulous summers. She made sure everything was right. We came first. My father was the same. They protected us from everything – to the stage that you'd think that the children in the top house in Pleasant View [where we lived] were recluses. If there was Bonfire Night we'd be in the house, we'd have fireworks in the back. Once we'd come out of Aberfan she made sure we were kept as a unit.

But, despite her efforts, there were always reminders.

> We lived in a street of 24 houses. We lost five little girls. And the school secretary was from the street as well. Nobody knew what the street was going through. But I know one thing. Phil walked that street every day. There was a reminder all the time. That's the part of the disaster... always someone will survive and someone will always remind you, or something will always remind you, and that's another emotion.

Though they lived in close proximity, one of the firemen who rescued Phil and Gerald Tarr, Len Haggett, had no desire afterwards to trace any of those he'd saved from the scene of the disaster.

> I don't know whether you blank your mind out as to what is going on, but I would not have been able to recognise the man we rescued from Moy Road although we were talking to him. I would not be able to recognise the young lad who was trapped under the stones. And I would not have been able to recognise the young girl that we rescued. And I've never met any of them to this day.
>
> I didn't want to go looking, in a sense. I once went down to the Gordon Lennox Club, where the children had been temporarily kept as a school. I went there with one of the other officers one day just to see what the situation was. But I didn't make any attempt to find out who the child was. I didn't want to cause her any pain. So I've never met them - to this day.

*

Schooling of a sort had resumed under the most difficult of circumstances thanks to the sterling efforts of the surviving teachers. A new primary school for Aberfan, Ynysowen, was finally opened in 1974 on a different site. Even so, there was inevitable disruption to the pattern and development of children's education and many of them found the return to school hard. Jeff Edwards, before the disaster a bright eight year-old, was one of those whose concentration was badly affected.

After the disaster they provided temporary accommodation for us – caravans basically – but it wasn't proper education, it was more play really. They didn't push us back into school, they let us find our own way back, and it wasn't really until my O Levels that I got back into education. Between the ages of eight and 14 we lost a lot of education in those important formative years.

My life totally changed after the disaster. I think my career path would probably have been different. I always wanted to be a doctor, that was my ambition, but having lost so much education in those formative years and found concentration so difficult... but I did get O and A levels, got a degree and a professional qualification in accountancy, so that hasn't held me back. I think others could have gone on to university, but because of their experience haven't been able to fulfil their career ambitions as they should have.

There were others whose education and life chances were affected by the disruption in their school lives and the after-effects of the disaster. Calvin Hodkinson had dug in vain trying to find his brother Royston, buried in his classroom. His senior school in Moy Road had been demolished in the Spring after the disaster and he had to start a new school elsewhere.

I moved to Afon Tâf high school then, in Abercynon and I just couldn't handle it.

I was bunking off, like, up the bank with a couple of my mates. [We were supposed to be] concentrating on our work, and I wasn't concentrating, I was just thinking...

Trying to write, we were doing Maths, and I like Maths. I can't remember the name of the teacher we had, a Miss it was, and she said, 'Calvin', she said, 'you're not concentrating!' And I thought, I can't tell her why. I was having flashbacks, digging, looking for my brother. I said no, I can't talk about the disaster at all to her.

So that was going on for weeks and weeks and weeks. They didn't know what I was going through at the time. I said [to my mother], 'Mam, I can't handle it up there, I'll be glad when I leave'. I think I was up there about a year and a half, I think I missed about eight months. I bunked off – just couldn't handle it at all up there. So I left then, by 15, and I was jumping from job to job.

Bernard Thomas too found it hard to cope with school and ended up with few qualifications.

My education has suffered. I ended up working in local factories making office equipment, filing cabinets etc. then as a machine operator in the Hoover factory for 14 years. Rather boring actually.

Phil Thomas had his own schooling problems. His head injury had induced memory loss.

I forgot how to read and write. I didn't go back to school till I was 13. So what my Mum and Dad used to do, we had so many letters from different schools at the time, hoping I'd get better and that, I used to write to a boy in Ireland, David. And his father was a doctor, and they used to make me write once a week. My Uncle Trev used to write the thing and I had to copy it to send out. I literally hated it... Nothing against David, but I just couldn't grasp the writing, the spelling and the reading.

And when I was 13 and I went to school I couldn't do the work they were doing so I was put down into a lower class then, with the thicko's, they used to tell us, like. But they were a great bunch of kids I went through school with, from all over the place.

*

But there were glimmers of hope for a community in recovery. Mary Davies saw the first signs.

In a very short time people realised you couldn't go on just doing nothing, so bit by bit, people got together, and tried to make a life in the village again.

The women of Aberfan made the first tentative moves. In the March of 1966, months before the disaster, Marilyn Brown had had an idea to mount a concert with the children of Aberfan. This was enthusiastically taken up by children and parents alike and preparations were already well in hand by October of that year. Then the disaster changed everything.

So when it happened, no-one wanted to bother, which was obvious, wasn't it? And Reverend Penberthy said to me one day, he said, 'Marilyn, why don't you carry on with the concert?' 'Oh', I said, 'I can't. I can't do that now, it wouldn't be right'. 'You do it', he said, 'never forget, there are other children need your help. And it would do you good'.

So I saw some of the Mums and yes, that would be alright, yes that would be fine, why not? So they told some of the children and we ended up with nearly 50 children. I helped them and they helped me. I think they helped me more than I helped them, they were absolutely fantastic. The Mums got together, the fathers got together. I had wonderful help, absolutely great help. And it helped them, you know, to get involved with things.

And the group of mothers who'd got together, we had meetings then, you know, and we did different things and had more than one glass and when we came out two of our members decided to cross the road and they were crossing the road without looking where they were going. And someone shouted, 'Really, Pam! You're not in Aberfan now. Get off the road!'

Laughter was at a premium and it helped with the healing process, as Marilyn remembers.

We had quite a few characters with the Wives. There was one lady, a rather large lady, and she always dressed up, and I think she helped a lot in this disaster because she made us laugh. You know, we cried and we laughed but she used to make us laugh because she'd dress up in the most silliest costumes going. We thought she was great and we enjoyed her company. There was one occasion – we were having a carnival – and she came to my husband - we had a couple of horses at the time – and she asked him if she could borrow a horse. And he said, 'What the devil for?' She said, 'Well, I'm going to dress up as Lady Godiva'. 'Oh my God', he said, 'you'll kill the blinkin' horse!' he said, 'I'm not lending you no horse!' And she eventually ended up sitting on the back of a Cadillac. She didn't care about anyone at all. She was great, and she kept us going as well. She was a character.

But the Wives weren't just about enjoying themselves. They came to see the group as a community resource. They started Meals on Wheels, a Keep Fit class, and raised money for good causes. They took part in carnivals and entertained elderly people in residential care homes. June felt it was incumbent on them, after the generosity shown to them by ordinary people after the disaster, to give something back.

We felt we were able to work for the community. We were active in those days, although we ranged from middle-30s to 70s in the group and there was no age limit either way. I remember it cost us a shilling a week, for which we had a cup of tea and money went into the fund. We helped out with refreshments at holiday camps, carnivals and [at a local community event] to celebrate the Investiture of Prince Charles [in 1969]. Any event, the group was large enough and capable enough to help out.

But we had wonderful times, really wonderful times. It helped us because I think we needed to leave our homes. We needed to meet together with people and I think... when we started we said we would try to give back to the local community, or nationwide, or world-wide in whatever way we could. Because we'd been through this terrible disaster we became much more sensitive to people in a similar or any sort of disaster – an earthquake or anything that had gone on in any part of the world – we felt differently about it because we'd got a pretty good idea of what they must be going through.

There were other benefits too. Mary believes it helped give her a confidence she'd never had before.

We had wonderful speakers that spoke to us in Wives, very influential people. And somebody always had to give the vote of thanks. It brought a lot of people out, including myself, to stand up and thank people – a Lord Lieutenant of Glamorgan, Chief Constables, anything. To be asked to stand up and give a vote of thanks when you're not used to public speaking is a lot. It brought me out. It did a lot for me. Because it was a different generation to today. We never went out but [to] our Wives group. I got a lot out of Wives. After I joined I went to college, joined a course down in Cardiff, part of the University. I don't think I'd ever have gone there if it hadn't been for Wives. So they've been good to me.

Most important perhaps, it was a place where bereaved mothers felt they could be themselves among friends.

> It was a marvellous group... there were a lot of people there that had lost children in the disaster and some had lost their homes. We felt that in the Wives we could talk about it, we could cry about it and we could laugh and no offence was taken. Do you understand? We helped each other. We helped each other. We had funny times together and we had very sad times together.

It was certainly a boon to founder-member Marilyn Brown.

> It definitely helped me. Because some of the women, some Mums who were coming, they'd lost children and they said themselves that it had helped them a lot. Because we didn't talk about it a lot, we didn't talk about the disaster, and wherever we went, I personally wouldn't say I was from Aberfan because we didn't want to talk about it. We do now. We used to say we were from Merthyr. But now we say we're from Aberfan. Because it's a long time, isn't it?

One of the positive legacies of the disaster, the Wives group is still going strong in Aberfan but memories of those early days of unaccustomed fun and much-needed companionship still burn bright.

The men of Aberfan weren't far behind. Though men had the comradeship of the pit and the factory, the pub and the club, it was always going to be more difficult in their male world of strength and stoicism to express emotion and share feelings after the disaster. Typically, men had coped by compartmentalising their experience, not talking about it, trying to shut it out. Even then emotions would occasionally break through in drink or during the still watches of the night.

One response was to reach back into the rich tradition of choral singing in Wales by founding a new choir. Like the Young

Wives, it chose to look outwards and to the future. The Aberfan Male Voice Choir (later renamed the Ynysowen Male Choir) started as a direct result of the disaster, founded by men – many of whom had lost loved ones – involved in the many meetings to press for the removal of the tips. It brought them together to raise money for charity by mounting concerts. It first met for twice-weekly practice in a local chapel, then at the new Ynysowen School when it opened in 1974. After a while, Aberfan's choir began to achieve national recognition, appearing on TV, performing concerts in Europe and singing for the Queen.

Like the Wives, it survives today as a positive legacy of the disaster, providing satisfaction and a social focus for its male choristers and great pleasure to its audiences in Wales and elsewhere. One of its founder members, now in his eighties, is still singing with them.

There was another positive coming together too, as Methodist lay preacher June Vaughan witnessed.

Since the disaster the word ecumenical has come into being. With the United Churches we meet once a month and then again during Lent and we share the big [religious] festivals, so we're together and we feel so lucky that this has come out of it. We hold this service on the day of the disaster. Seven o'clock in the evening and we go round each church in turn [each year]. We understand if some people feel more secure in their own homes but there are 70 people who want to come and meet together on the evening of that day. Different people from all the churches will take part in it. Sometimes the people are local, sometimes they've moved out of the area and it's good to see them again.

*

A physical legacy was always planned for the money raised from the disaster fund. The distinctive rows of the original

Portland stone arches above the graves of 88 of the children in Bryntaf and the landscaping, planting and upkeep of the children's memorial section of the cemetery and a small memorial garden nearby were its first manifestation. But it was many years before the main 'bricks and mortar' legacies were available to the people of Aberfan.

A new Community Centre was opened by the Queen in March 1973. This was her second but not her last visit to Aberfan. Jeff Edwards, then a teenager, was there and like many in the village, he values the personal interest she has always taken.

> We've been lucky here in Aberfan because the Queen has taken a real interest in the community. She came here 10 days after the disaster itself, so that she could see the aftermath. She was very emotionally upset after visiting the cemetery... Obviously she met families during that day and a lot of them expressed how, as a mother not a queen, she was sympathetic with their losses and the difficulties they were facing as young parents, as she was. Then she came back here for the opening of the Community Centre, built from the proceeds of the disaster fund – people from all over the world contributed. I was at High School then.

The new primary school at Ynysowen opened the following year, and a memorial garden was built on the site of the demolished Pantglas School, tracing the layout of the original hall and classrooms with low stone walls, and filled with flowers and young trees. A new memorial playground, known locally as the Coventry Park and paid for by donations from the people of that city and opened by its Mayor in 1972, was built on the site of the old Merthyr Vale School elsewhere in the village. Another, smaller, playground was built next to the memorial garden on the site of eight houses on the west side of Moy Road destroyed by the tip.

*

More personal and individual forms of remembrance became part of the fabric of survivors' lives. Karen Thomas had lost two dear cousins in the disaster but she had survived. She soon came to recognise the debt she owed to the school meals clerk Nansi Williams, who had shielded her and four other children in the school hall, and she wanted to do something about it.

> At twelvemonth after [the disaster] we were going up [to the cemetery] because I had my own pot on Angela and Stephen and we were going up to put flowers up there, and as we were going up the hill Mam said Nansi was buried there and I said I wanted to put flowers there. And we done that every year on October 21st. No-one knew that I was doing it. Nansi's mother came into the shop [where my mother worked] and said to Mam one year, 'I don't know', she said, 'every time I go up there, someone's been there before me and is putting flowers on Nansi and I can't seem to find out who it is'. After a while, Mam told her it was me.

She also kept in touch with Nansi's family.

> I knew her husband, because on my 18th birthday he came up to the house and he brought me a present. It was a little silver trinket box in the shape of a piano and it played music. And I still have that. I treasure that.

There were other, more novel, ways of memorialising the dead. Denise Morgan lost her sister Annette. Her father, who she recalls hearing sobbing into his pillow for months after the disaster, had a special way of remembering his daughter that the family all came to appreciate.

> We had some money given to us after the disaster, and I think one of the things my father wanted to do was to try and get us back to normal, as a family, as normal family

life as possible. For the first time, we went down to Porthcawl. He said to me – I can see his face now – he said to me, 'What do you think of this caravan Denise?' I said, 'I'm not fussy on the colour,' and as we walked around the front of the caravan, there was a big sign in the middle of the window. My sister's name was in the front of the caravan – they'd named the caravan *Annette*. And he said, 'Well, it's ours!' Well, it was just so much excitement then!

Calvin Hodkinson lost his beloved younger brother Royston. Much later, when his first son was born, the baby's name seemed a foregone conclusion.

I said to my wife, 'I do really want to name him Royston, after my brother'. 'Yes', she said, 'I'm fine by that'. I said I'm going to have to ask my mother, so I called my mother, and I said, 'Do you mind if I name him Royston?' Oh, she grabbed hold of me, hugging me, 'Yes', she said, 'I don't mind at all'. I think she was really pleased. It was her first grandchild and all, and his name was Royston, and oh, she spoilt him rotten, she did. I think it got her out of her shell when her first grandkid came along, it got her out of her shell a bit.

*

Some survivors and bereaved families chose not to stay in Aberfan but to seek a fresh start far away. A few emigrated. At 18 Jeff Edwards made the decision to move away. The village he'd grown up in now held nothing for him but painful memories.

I left Aberfan to improve my life. I went to London to university and remained there for a while.

He got a good degree, qualified as an accountant and made a successful career. Much later, on return visits to the village, he was shocked by what he found. By this time the mass pit closures of the 1980s had had a devastating impact on the old South Wales coalfield. The valleys were full of redundant mines and redundant men put on long-term sickness benefit to disguise the true level of unemployment. Merthyr Vale colliery had managed to keep open against all odds until 1989, but by the early 1990s the impact of its absence was only too evident. Jeff found a despondent place trapped in a dependent culture.

> When I came back to the village I saw young people who would traditionally have gone into the mining industry and would have worked their way through to become electrical engineers or mining engineers [but] the closure of the mines left a huge void in the community. We had a generation who were lost, who had left school with no qualifications. They couldn't read, they couldn't write. What an indictment on society in this day and age. A third of our children were in that situation. What came over to me from these young people was the hopelessness and despair in their lives caused by the boredom and not having the dignity of employment, turning to alcohol and drugs to alleviate that boredom. So I was determined to come back and help those young people.

Jeff was strongly motivated by what he saw and it linked back to his own experience of the disaster and the success he'd made of his own life since leaving Aberfan. This was the positive flipside to the nagging survivor's guilt he had often felt.

> I'd done very well, so when I came back and saw these young people with no hope and no future I felt a duty to try to help them achieve something in their own lives. Because to me, it was another waste of life and the disaster of 1966 took away the lives of so many young people that

could have made a huge contribution to society had they lived. To those who survived, I think it's incumbent on them to help this area, which has suffered so much in terms of social and economic deprivation since the demise of the coal industry.

So he returned to live in the area in 1994 and set about making determined efforts to make a difference.

When I came back, I saw a lot of young people hanging about on the streets drinking flagons of cider, getting off their heads on drugs, stealing cars, stripping them down, selling off the parts to buy drugs and alcohol. There was a lot of concern in the village about these youngsters causing bedlam, so I got in contact with a number of local residents who were interested in engaging with these people.

Like that other community initiative many years before, the Young Wives, Jeff's work started in insalubrious accommodation under a church.

With the local Presbyterian minister we started out in the basement of a chapel in Merthyr. There was fungus growing out of the walls. About 30 of these young people were huddled round this gas fire. What came out was that they had left school, no qualifications, no self-esteem, no motivation, unable to read or write. So I got a group of people from the local Council, from the police and from the local community there and 25 of those young people put their hands up. They didn't want skating rinks or bowling alleys, they wanted to be able to read and write. So we got grants, the first one was from Children in Need, for a venue and a community worker.

From a small project, we built an organisation that employed 45 people and had a turnover of nearly £1million a year, providing interventions to help young people. We refurbished Trinity Chapel, so we then had a purpose-built centre to engage with them. We looked at literacy skills, computing skills, raising self-esteem and competence. What we found was that a lot of children were having children – 13 and 14 year-old kids, one minute they had a doll, next minute they had a real child. They didn't have any parenting skills, no means of dealing with a newborn child, so we started parenting classes.

We put on courses to help raise their educational attainment, then we went out to employers to persuade them to take these young people on. We knew they were very interested in cars and stripping cars, so at the back of the Chapel we built a garage, teaching motor mechanics and maintenance. These kids loved that. They weren't academic by any standard but we devised an open learning course on manual competences so at the end they could have a paper qualification and that made a hell of a difference to their self-esteem and motivation because they could go out to an employer and say, well, I've got these skills and here's the piece of paper to prove it. Lots of employers in the Merthyr area were very supportive and to this day we have people employed there who've come through the project.

We found one of the barriers to employment in South Wales was transport, and that was particularly true after 6pm. So we set up a car-to-employment scheme, with the young people servicing the cars under supervision. We made a pact with school refusers that if they came to the project to work on the cars, they'd spend two days a week in school.

We bought a derelict cafe in the centre of the village, we renovated it with European funding, and we brought the first cyber cafe to Merthyr Tydfil. The Megabytes Cafe in Aberfan provided affordable meals and in the basement we had this computer suite and we taught computer skills to enhance their employability. It was one of the best projects we undertook really because it brought two dimensions of the village together – the elderly people who didn't understand computers but had very good social skills, and young people with good computer skills but their social skills weren't as good. Two parts of the community who were once at loggerheads were brought together and ended up helping each other and a mutual understanding of each other's problems so there was a greater tolerance of what had been happening and why.

One thing led to another: there was a Dial-a-Ride scheme to get people without transport to surgeries, supermarkets and hospital appointments. As a result, immunisation rates went up and feelings of isolation broke down, old friendships were renewed and new ones were made. All these schemes initiated by Jeff and others in the Merthyr area made a positive difference in many people's lives.

As a result of his community work Jeff was, perhaps inevitably, drawn into local politics. He was elected as an Independent for Mid-Glamorgan County Council and became a Cabinet member for finance, economic development and regeneration on Merthyr Tydfil Council. In 2005 he was elected Centenary Mayor of Merthyr Tydfil. He took this opportunity to sell Merthyr, not as a declining, dependent area but one coming to terms with post-industrialisation and a good place to visit and to invest. One of his proudest achievements is that, as a result of the inward investment attracted, unemployment figures – for years among the highest in the country – had reversed by the time he left office.

The disaster survivor who couldn't wait to get away from Aberfan in his youth returned three decades later as an adult to give exceptional service to the area and has left a lasting and positive legacy. This has given Jeff Edwards great personal and professional satisfaction.

Public service has been important to me, more so than accountancy. Had I known about community development before, I wouldn't have gone into accountancy as a profession, I would have gone into community work, because the power of that for change is so important.

Another returnee from London was Mansel Aylward, who'd left well before the disaster to study medicine.

I was determined I was going to be one of these heroic surgeons, you know, cutting things out and doing wonderful things because I was addicted to *Doctor Kildare* and *Ben Casey* and all that.

But his experiences at the scene and with bereaved families shortly afterwards changed his mind. He returned to Merthyr in 1969 and became a GP in nearby Dowlais. Here he saw first hand how the after-shocks of the disaster had affected his patients.

I realised, having witnessed that terrible event and being involved with the people who were my patients thereafter, that I didn't want to do that sort of work, I wanted to look into why people became ill, what effect that had on their lives, and what interventions we could do apart from drugs which would help people return to a more normal way of life. I realised that depression and health in general – not just mental health but their physical health – was determined by their social background, by their thoughts, by their beliefs, and that was a way by which one could tackle depression in a much more useful way.

Aberfan began a series of unrelated, unexpected events in my life which changed the way I thought about medicine. I went from being an adherent of the medical model – the body is just a machine and illness is just the machine gone wrong – it's more than that. It's more about understanding the way people think, believe, and are influenced by their society.

He went on to study depression and the effects of trauma on health. Now Professor Sir Mansel Aylward, he has advised government departments and chaired public health bodies. He is currently Director of the Centre for Psychosocial Research, Occupational and Physician Health at the University of Cardiff School of Medicine. Aberfan, he says, 'changed my working life and my home life'.

> Having now done work on what are the factors that promote health and wellbeing, number one is the relationships with other people. That overarches any other factors. Money is not that important. So it's changed the ways I've thought about the successes we can see in medicine and many of them are not medical issues, drug advancements, it's improvements in the way in which we relate to each other. And I never thought of that until I witnessed Aberfan and the aftermath.

*

There were positive national legacies left by the Aberfan disaster too. The Tribunal report identified gaps and whole chasms in safety legislation governing tipping from mines. As a result the Mines and Quarries (Tips) Act was passed in 1969. And in response to Davies' devastating indictment of NCB's management oversight – or lack of it – of its activities' risks to employees and members of the public, a committee was established in 1970 by Barbara Castle, Secretary of State for Employment and Productivity. It reported in 1972 and its recommendations resulted in the Health and Safety at Work etc Act 1974, legislation that has guided health and safety policy ever since.

The Committee's Chairman was none other than Lord Alfred Robens. By then he'd left the National Coal Board. During his tenure he'd overseen the Labour government's massive pit closure programme, far bigger than that of the 1980s under Margaret Thatcher which precipitated the 1984 miners' strike.

Of the almost 700 mines when he took office in 1961 there were less than 300 by the time he left in 1971 and the number of miners employed by the NCB had been cut by half.

But Robens' later good works on health and safety couldn't save his reputation, tarnished irreparably by Aberfan.

7

Moving On

Aberfan today bears little resemblance to the dirty monochrome images of 1966. The village is still a huddle of long terraces and narrow streets though many of its shops and pubs, bustling and alive with gossip in the 1960s, are long gone. Gone too is Merthyr Vale Colliery, in its place green landscaping and – appropriately enough – a fine new primary school opened by the Queen in 2012.

The River Taff still winds along the valley floor, now clean and teeming with fish, crossed by a new road linking one side of the valley with the other. Once defaced by seven black tips, the surrounding mountains are uniformly green again. The only relic of what once was the lifeblood of the place – and its tormentor – is the wheel of the old pit winding gear, now sunk in the ground as the centrepiece of a new roundabout. These days Aberfan is altogether a quieter, greener place.

The magnet for activity now is not the colliery but the Community Centre where families have weekend fun in the big hall, children swim, people work out in the gym, retired folk seek gentler pursuits in the Library and small boys snack on chips in the cafe. There's a lot going on here. The Coventry Park playground, condemned as unfit on health and safety grounds, now has bungalows built over it but the playground in Moy Road lives on, shabby but well-used.

In high summer the Memorial Garden next door, where Pantglas Junior School once stood, is serene and full of colour:

phlox, astilbes, montbretia, hydrangea – and rosemary for Remembrance. The trees are now growing to maturity, small spring-flowering trees, among them one planted by the Queen on her third visit in 1997. High up behind the garden and playground on the old railway bank, the Taff Trail is busy with dog-walkers, cyclists and ramblers. You can now walk from the Beacons to Cardiff on the Trail through beautiful countryside once despoiled but now reclaimed.

It is funded by, among others, the European Union and something called the Coal Authority. This ghostly successor to the NCB was set up in 1994 to 'manage the effects of past coal mining'. The Taff Trail is one triumphant legacy of the otherwise painful demise of coal in the Welsh valleys.

*

Bryntaf burial ground just outside the village is the solemn place it always was. Set on the steep hillside, its older headstones lean and stagger. Even on the brightest summer day it is exposed and austere. The Aberfan children's section is a climb from the entrance towards the top of the cemetery but its rows of white arches are visible from miles around. The more so now: they shine out. After nearly 50 years the original Portland stone had badly deteriorated. A major refurbishment programme was started in 2008, renewing the arches in sparkling granite and re-engraving all the monumental masonry. The small adjacent memorial garden was restored too and replanted in a pink and blue scheme to represent the girls and boys lying nearby. The children are now gradually being joined by their mothers and fathers, as was their wish. Calvin Hodkinson had made a promise to his parents.

My mother always said to me, 'You promise me when I pass away, I want to be with Royston'. So I said, 'Yes, I promise you'. My father passed away in July 2009. He's gone in with my brother. My mother then she was devastated, and she'd been married 50 odd years. That was July. November then, my mother passed away, she was just heartbroken. And she's in with my brother and all. My mother, my father and my brother in the same grave. It's so hard.

After 50 years the children's cemetery is a pristine place and a sad place. For some it's too sad a place to visit. Karen Thomas will continue to lay flowers on Nansi Williams' grave but she can go no further.

> I goes up to the cemetery to put flowers on her, because she isn't with the children, so I am able to just go up as far as her and put flowers there because that's the only way I can thank her. I will never be able to thank her enough for saving us and I will always go up and put flowers there. No-one knows I go up there, I go up there on my own. I can't go up the top to the children part of the cemetery. I used to when I was little but the older I got... I can't go up there. I haven't been up to Angela and Stephen for about 25, 30 years. I can't go up there.

*

The disaster fund and its subsequent offshoot charities, depleted by time and many disbursements, could no longer bear the expense of such a major undertaking as the wholesale renewal of the children's cemetery. The situation looked hopeless. To avert further distress to the bereaved and secure continuity of care for all the memorials, in 2007 the Welsh Assembly stepped in with a grant of £1.5million to the Aberfan Memorial Charity to enable the work to be done.

Though it was never made explicit, this was roughly the amount represented by interest forgone on the £150,000 taken – some say fraudulently – from the disaster fund in 1968 for the removal of the tips. The capital sum had finally been repaid to the fund in 1997 as one of the first acts of the incoming Labour government after years of local lobbying. It was the very least they could do and it was a long time coming. And now the longstanding and outstanding debt, the cause of so much bitterness in Aberfan, has at last been repaid in full.

*

The dead are still remembered in hearts and homes. Marilyn Brown has a little remembrance ritual.

> We've got quite a lot of photographs [of Janette] around the house and we've got one in the bedroom. Every night when I go to bed I just touch it. I touch her photograph and I say goodnight. We've also got one in the hall and I touch that every time I pass. I don't know, it gives me a sense of 'she's still with us'. Yes, that feeling of, yes, I do remember you and I will always remember you.

She finds solace at the chapel where Janette and many of the other children went to Sunday School.

> The children went to a little Methodist chapel. It was tiny. Quite a lot of the children went to Sunday School so it was quite a nice little group, they were always friends together. But they called it Tommy Small's chapel, it wasn't known as anything else. I think a lot of the little chapel because the children went there and we did a lot of things, you know, nativity plays... I still feel that it belongs to those children, you know, it's always near to my heart and I love going there. Not as a service, but to go into the chapel – it always gives me a good feeling, it helps me.

Inevitably, people still wonder what if and what might have been.

[Janette] would have been 61 now and I think, what would she have been like now? What would she have done?

It's a common thread for those who have lost those dear to them. Karen Thomas still misses the friendship with her cousin Angela.

I often wonder, would my life be any different? I think it would have been different and what we would have been doing. I don't think I'd be alone like I am now.

Others now alone, like Bernard Thomas, also wonder what if?

I wonder what I'd be had it not have happened. Would I have been married, living together or whatever? [I] didn't want to get too attached to one person. Trust perhaps... lost me self-confidence, especially as a kid.

Hettie Taylor thinks about what might have been for the children she'd taught at Pantglas in her first year who were lost.

I don't know what Lynn and Julie would have gone on to do but they were very clever girls, pretty girls too. They were good at athletics, they were good at netball. They were good academically, they were all-rounders.

And of her young colleagues who died.

...thinking about people like Michael and Madge, they'd only just started teaching. Madge had got married in the summer and her future in front of her and having children... It was all wiped up because of this slurry.

Painful memories, old symptoms, sometimes resurface. A TV programme or news of a disaster somewhere in the world will stir long-suppressed feelings. For Gloria Davies

...certain things arise sometimes out of the blue and especially if you see something on television, and then it comes back again. It will never ever go away. It will always be raw, even after 50 years.

Small things can trigger bad memories. For Joyce Hughes it is cut flowers and fog.

We had so many flowers in that week, that I just can't have flowers in the house now... Every time we have mist come down in the street, I can think, she was going down that morning and it was all foggy and I was trying to push her to hurry up, to go to school, and then that happened... Every time we have fog and it's in the streets and it's down, you think of it then.

There are more distressing manifestations for some. Karen Thomas still has nightmares.

I can see myself being buried in the nightmares and sometimes when I wake up I can feel myself pulling at Nansi's hair. I have hot sweats. Sometimes I wake up and I'm reeling. I just shoot out of bed and I don't know where I am. You know, the nightmares are really vivid. And I have them quite regular.

Anniversaries can be difficult for her too.

I don't like October. At all. When October 1st come in I go very quiet. We try and go away sometimes, we quite often go away on holiday, we tend to make it late September, October. And then on the anniversary I try not to be in the area. I'll go away for the day. Or if I'm at home I don't leave the house. I've got a friend, she texts me every year to tell me she's thinking of me.

They are a time for reflection, sadness, but also for drawing on memories of happier times. Hettie goes to the Memorial Garden where her school once stood.

> For me, on the anniversary, I go to the school, I don't go to the cemetery. For me... [*cries*], the school was where the children were and where they were happy. If I go to the school, I can hear their voices and hear them. I don't want to remember them in the cemetery. I want to remember them happy in the school, and for me, that's where I go. I can hear their voices, I can hear their happiness in the school. They were happy while they lived and that's the main thing. I've got my memories there. I don't want to remember them in their coffins [*crying*] I want to remember them playing and laughing. When I go to the school I can see my classroom and I can see my children. Oh, they were lovely children. So bright, there was something special about them. They were... and that's where that comes to me.

Many believe that injury or loss has, against all odds, given them something positive in their lives. Joyce Hughes' daughter Denise Morgan was awarded an MBE for her work as a Head Teacher in a tough school in Merthyr.

> Losing my sister in the disaster made me a much stronger person, because I went on to become a teacher, and I worked for a long time in a socially deprived area, and I think it made me understand traumas that children go through, upsets that children go through, and I think I was able to empathise with that really, and that's one of the reasons I stayed, I think, so long in my last post before I retired. I could feel for children when they had lost someone that was close to them, and I just feel like I had something to offer them, in some sort of way, understanding what they were going through.

Even severe injuries and the removal of three fingers on his right hand hasn't held Phil Thomas back from making the most of his life.

It's never stopped me doing anything. I enjoy life. I don't dwell on Aberfan. It's sad, it upsets me, but I think my Mam done such a good job, it doesn't affect me. I used to get the odd nightmare, but I haven't had them for years now. I always feel sad coming up to the anniversary, doesn't matter which one it is. But it's never stopped me doing anything.

It was hard when I had to start to write again, 'cos they said, 'Left hand! Left hand!' I always went back to the right hand. I play darts with my right hand. I play bowls right hand. I play ten-pin bowling – chucks the ball down, sticks my thumb in. It hasn't stopped me doing nothing. When the nurses said, yes, you have lost your fingers, I think that was the shock. Now, I don't miss 'em. I'd rather be without 'em than with 'em. And that's the truth that is. I wouldn't know what to do if I had bloody 10 fingers! [*Laughing*] I wouldn't! I would not know what to do.

As his brother Alan says, their relationship – and the love and support they had from their parents – sustains them both.

Phil, there's a love between me and Philip [*emotional*].... if he's there, he's there. If he isn't I know where he is. And the feeling is the same, mutual, both ways. If he has a problem, he comes to see me and if I have a problem I go to see him. We've had a few in our lifetime. And a lot of scrapes, a lot of fun, a lot of happy memories.

Yes, life is moving on. He has his grandchildren now, exciting time for him. He can't run as fast as he used to though! His grandson Thomas winds him up and I have to laugh because I can see my father in him – he used to be full of fun and wickedness. They were really wonderful parents. I can't say no more than that... By the time he was 18, Philip was married, so he moved out. And by the time he was 22 he had four children, he was well into fatherhood. But we played darts, and we also started sea fishing, so we done a lot of sea fishing together and the Aberfan Social Club started a sea angling club there... so we spent a lot of time together that way. ... But the bond is always there. We know where each other is, and that bond will never be taken from us I don't think. We've had a rollercoaster. We've had a good life and I hope it continues a lot longer.

Children who arrived after 1966 have brought light into the lives of bereaved families. After Janette died Marilyn Brown still had her son Robert and didn't think she would have any more children. Then she and Bernard went on to have two more girls.

After the disaster I never thought about having any more children. When Lynne was born... she was great, a lovely child, really small and pretty and dainty. And then Jayne came out of the blue really and I think she's paid me back for that because she does everything that I couldn't possibly do – climbs mountains and I don't know what else. She's my gardener by the way. Lynne's my hairdresser and Robert's my painter and decorator, so I haven't done so bad! [*Laughs*]

I think I'm lucky because I had two more children for a start. And the way they've turned out, I was blessed with them. It was meant to be, probably, wasn't it? They were my help, they were my strength when you think about it.

Adult survivor Gerald Tarr too discovered happy times when he and his wife Shirley had a family of their own.

It was years after the disaster I started a family of my own. Things seemed to settle down in the village. For a long time the village was empty of children. But when I started having children loads of people were having kids, and the village gradually filled up with children. It was great to see children running about the place and of course the village settled down a bit and the place did eventually come back to life.

It was marvellous, having children. Of course you're more protective after something like that happened. You want to know where they go, what they're doing, what bus they catch. 'Cos you're so worried about them, don' you? We enjoyed the kids, because my wife she loved kids, you know. They were good times in my life. We used to have marvellous times at Christmas with the kids. We used to look forward to Christmas then. We had lovely times. I used to cook a turkey for her. We had good times. We used to see a bit of snow in them days too – kids used to go out playing in the snow and I got a little pony for her [daughter] a little white horse and we used to put them on a sleigh and get the horse to get the loaf of bread or the milk when the snow was down. I used to learn her to ride then, on the horses, she took to it natural like. I used to ride anything when I was a kid, used to break horses in and everything. She had a little pony and when she grew out of it we bought her a bigger horse then. Oh, we had a great time with the kids.

*

The Wives still meet in Aberfan, a smaller group now and, as Mary Morse says ruefully, no longer young.

But of course now, we're not the Young Wives no more. We call ourselves Wives – we'd have a cheek to call ourselves Young Wives because we're more like Old Age

Pensioners! We're only about 26 on the books now, but the culture's changed. The generation has changed, see? It wouldn't interest the young people, what interested us. But the Wives give us a lot of comfort. A lot of pleasure and a lot of comfort.

Gloria Davies agrees, and she still enjoys it today.

It's helped us no end! We meet every Wednesday, and we either get a speaker, or somebody does a party. When I say a party, a jewellery party or make-up party or whatever, oh but then we'd go to see a show or get together with something-or-another, some function...

For June Vaughan it represents friendships forged in adversity that have lasted a lifetime.

In the Wives we're 24 now and we're Friends with a capital F. So because we've been helped so much we believe we have to give back something of what we've been given. We are privileged, inasmuch as we have come together – not everyone, we understand why some people don't join the group, they don't want to do it, they don't feel the need – but there are so many that do.

The group may be smaller but it still serves an important function for founder-member Marilyn Brown.

The numbers have dwindled, we're getting older. Quite a few of us are quite old but there are younger people coming along. And I think we still enjoy each other's company. I have a lot of joy... out of my friends. Well, we've all helped one another over the years. And we always will do. Always will do.

*

When he was interviewed, Len Haggett said he had never met any of the three people he had helped rescue with fellow fireman Dave Thomas 50 years ago. And Phil Thomas had no idea who had lifted his head clear of the deluge from the water main and then dragged him from the rubble in Moy Road.

After their respective interviews were recorded, Phil, Len and Dave were reunited for the first time on camera for the BBC documentary, *Surviving Aberfan*. Phil was finally able to thank his rescuers and Len and Dave were able to see the results of their efforts in robust good health. It was a touching moment of genuine warmth. If Len has a lasting regret it is that he and his colleagues were able to get so few out alive.

In his interview Len explained at some length why he hadn't wanted, or been able, to talk about his role in the disaster in the past, and why he had decided to tell his story now. This was a common theme, especially among the men. It seems that the women of Aberfan had found it easier in some ways to come to terms with what happened and so had less difficulty in talking as time eased the pain. It was different for many of the men, who preferred to try and forget something that essentially could never be forgotten. Deciding to talk at all, much less to a potential audience of millions, cost much personal anguish.

> I didn't want to fetch it back in my memory. I didn't want to tell [my wife] Barbara what I'd seen down there, what I'd been involved with. And, you know, my feelings were for the children and families involved. I lived in Aberfan, I knew a number of the parents who lost children there. I didn't want to meet them; they had more than enough pain to deal with. And that's one of the reasons why I never spoke about it before. You push it into the back of your memory. And unfortunately, knowing that I'd have to talk about it, I've thought about it over the past couple of days and brought them memories back into my mind and you can picture what was there. And they're not pleasant memories.

My first reaction was, no, I don't want to discuss it. I don't want to open wounds for the parents who've lost children and the other families. And probably I didn't want to open the memories that were in the back of my mind.

So I put [the television company's invitation] away for a while and then in January I thought about it, pulled it out and put it away and thought about it and put it away. And then I did realise that if we don't say that we know what happened, then it will never be known. Many of the officers who were there that day, colleagues of mine, have now gone, passed on. All of the Junior Officers have died, quite a few of the firemen at the time. And I felt that what the [invitation] said was quite true, that the involvement of the Fire Service, though known and accepted and acknowledged, should be recorded somewhere along the way. Maybe as a lesson for others, I don't know, but that was my feelings.

I've always been proud of the Fire Service and I still am proud of the Fire Service. And I felt that one of the first emergency services to arrive and to be able to carry out rescues ... I'm well aware that the teachers in the school and people living in the vicinity of the school helped in the rescue before we arrived, because it was probably five or 10 minutes from the time we received the call to the time we arrived in Aberfan and children had been rescued and removed from the school before us. But no-one had really discussed what the Fire Service involvement was, probably for the reasons I said, you know, they were too painful to discuss; they didn't want to. People have got their own way of dealing with things, whether it's to go in the corner and have a cry on your own, because counselling didn't exist in those days – you dealt with it in the best way that you could.

I don't know, that probably is the reason why I decided to do the interview and talk to you about it. And probably

– I hope – it will go back in my memory. It will never be erased, but it will go back into the background and not be as painful and traumatic as it has been, thinking about it over the past couple of days and knowing that I would have to discuss it with you and knowing that my thoughts and my actions would be recorded.

How did Len feel about finally telling his story?

I feel that it's right to talk about it, so that it is recorded. I don't know that talking about it to you will make me feel any better. It will not remove the memories that are there. I can't leave here and say, 'Oh, I feel a lot better now I've talked about it'. I don't know that I will. I may well do in a week's time, in a month's time, in a year's time, I don't know. But at this present moment in time it may have helped to talk about it and say what had happened, but then I don't think I'm going to discuss it in detail again. I don't believe that I will. It's too traumatic and it's too painful.

But it is part of history. Not very pleasant history but like all history it should be recorded and people should know what happened that day, what individuals done, what the majority of people done, what was done from the Fire Service point of view. We were proud of what we did. We were only sorry that we couldn't have done more. But if you don't speak to the people who were actually there, you'll never have a record of what happened.

Some had chosen not to speak over the years out of respect for the bereaved – many of whom have now passed away. At the time and for many years after, Gerald Tarr was conscious of the pain that could be caused to parents of the dead children.

I've waited 50 years to give these interviews because I wouldn't give 'em. At the time there's papers knocking at my door, asking for interviews. I wouldn't give any. But after 50 years I will talk about it now. And the reason for that is, if the mothers and fathers is reading what I went through, they might have thought that their kids went through it, you know? I wouldn't have wanted them to know that their children were struggling and not being able to breathe. I wouldn't want their mothers and fathers to think I was dying or was praying to die because I knew I was dying slow. I didn't want them to think of what their own kids, what they went through. So that's why I wouldn't give interviews till now. There you are.

David Hopkins is still not prepared to talk in detail to his mother, especially about his feelings of guilt about being kept at home while his brother and sister died in the school.

I haven't told this story many times, because there's been no need to tell it, I don't think even my Mam has heard this story, because I don't think it's right to tell her. She knows bits, but I don't think it's right to tell her all of it.

Brothers Phil and Alan Thomas always respected their mother's wish that the disaster and Phil's part in it should never be spoken of – in the house or outside it. When she died this constraint was finally lifted.

She passed away 12 months ago and I think it would be nice that Philip and I done something together that will be remembered and that'll be it, Aberfan will be out of our consciousness.

That perhaps is doubtful. Alan's testimony was extraordinarily detailed and emotional. Making it was obviously something of a trial for him but he has given posterity a uniquely moving record of his own and his brother's experience of the disaster – and of the love and strength of their family life in childhood and beyond.

As a community leader, Jeff Edwards recognises more than most the untold personal cost of giving such public interviews.

> I know people in this community who, to this very day, have still not come to terms with what happened. It's so, so difficult for them to speak about it without getting so emotionally distraught, it's so raw to them, as if it was yesterday. It's all very well for TV crews and reporters to come to the community, and we get it on each and every anniversary, and the people give their stories, but they don't understand the turmoil that causes to that individual once they've gone. They've expressed their feelings, but they don't pick the pieces up afterwards. Somebody said it's like being raped... and that's why many people won't talk about what happened on the day.

But he takes a different view.

> So why do I talk about it? I always found it therapeutic and I say it because I want to raise awareness for people that, if you are involved in a major tragedy, it's not the end of your life. You can make a contribution to society after. You don't have to close everything down, which people often do. Their lives are centred around themselves and they can't see further than that.
>
> I think one of the important occasions was when the Queen came to Aberfan [in 1997]. After that visit we all went to the Castle Hotel in Merthyr Tydfil. A number of survivors and also teachers who'd survived were there and for the very first time, those individuals spoke about what happened on that day, and that was 30 years after. And they found that therapeutic because they'd brought issues that had been at the back of the subconscious to the front and as a result, they had a better understanding of their feelings.

I suffer from bouts of depression and I've found that talking about these things helps tremendously because it releases from your subconscious those things that many people have hidden away, been unable to speak about, and that's not because they don't want to speak about them. It's because they can't.

June Vaughan knows that talking isn't easy, but she has a more benign view of the media coming to Aberfan to hear people's stories.

I've heard no criticism whatsoever about the way we've been interviewed or... by the media. They've been absolutely wonderful. We don't look forward to talking, believe it or not [*laughs*]. We don't look forward to it at all. We all have sleepless nights thinking, well, what can we say? You know, what else can you say about it? But it's been wonderful. We were amazed that so many people came to us, wanted to talk to us, wanted to help us. We were completely amazed. We're amazed that you are here [*to interviewer*] and doing so much work after all this time.

*

Fifty years on in Aberfan the bereaved, survivors, rescue workers and all those who volunteered so tirelessly at the scene have found their own ways of dealing with the experience and the memories and feelings it left behind. Some have coped more successfully than others. Personality plays its part: some people are more instinctively optimistic than others but strong family ties and social networks – existing or wrought from the disaster – have helped many who were otherwise isolated or floundering. Talking about it released some from the torment of trying to keep painful thoughts at bay. Resolutely suppressing those thoughts worked for some up to a point, though for everyone we spoke to the disaster is an indelible part of their lives.

Whether they wish it or not, it will always be with them. As
Gloria Davies says: 'Until I die I suppose'.

There is residual anger directed against the long-gone Coal
Board. Former miner Gerald Tarr's post-disaster problems with
the effects of tipping haven't softened his view.

> I feel hateful for what they got away with. They got away
> with killing all them children. And they done it, oh yes.
> Only them. They didn't check the probers. They didn't
> check the dumping. And that's why the disaster happened.
> Through the NCB. They got away with everything. That
> made me mad. It makes me mad now, isn't it, to think
> they got away with everything.

He still wrestles with a tangle of strong memories and strong
emotions.

> I'll be honest with you, I weren't so ill that I can't
> remember like it was yesterday. Still, I'm alright now. But
> do you know, if I could have saved one of those kids I'd
> go through it a dozen times. If I could just save one.
> [*Upset*] That's the truth.

Others take a pragmatic view. For Alan Thomas, keeping it in
public memory is the important thing.

> You can beat yourself up over if and what, and where and
> why for the rest of your life and you'd still come out and
> you wouldn't have an answer for Aberfan... It's the fact,
> and I think it will never be forgotten. It's 1966. England
> won the World Cup. 1966, Aberfan disaster. It will never
> be forgotten. That day will never be forgotten.

Yet what is striking from these interviews is the positivity that
shines from much of the testimony, even from those who
suffered great injury or loss. Salvation Army volunteer Dorothy
Burns saw it for herself.

A whole generation of children went in that disaster, but Aberfan picked itself up and they've got on with their life, but it's something you'll never, never forget. Never. Never.

Marilyn Brown has been and remains upbeat.

If it's me, I'd rather laugh than cry. And I like to see other people laughing too, I like to make other people laugh as well. Maybe sometimes I'm a bit stupid, but there you are [*laughs*]. Other people have different ways of looking at this but we loved to entertain and that and I think that definitely helped us all the way along the line.

There is still immense pride in their area, their village and their community. Through his regeneration and community work, Jeff Edwards has come to believe Merthyr and its environs has great potential.

We still have an important role in the life of the nation... And we live in such a beautiful area. When I was growing up the river was black with the washing of the coal and the tips were so high you couldn't see the sun. You talk about dark satanic mills, well, all of that has gone. We live in such a naturally beautiful area with walks along the Taff Trail and walks along the Beacons at the head of the valley. So as Leader, and as Mayor, it gave me great pride to sell Merthyr as a great place to live, work and to play.

Marilyn's friend Mary Morse is still there and wouldn't live anywhere else.

Aberfan is a wonderful village. And I think the people are wonderful in the village and it's a wonderful community. Because I'm disabled at the moment and not enjoying good health but not a day goes by somebody doesn't knock on my door: 'Do you want anything, Mary?' Now you don't get that everywhere, do you? So to me, I think Aberfan is a wonderful place and the friends I have here.

I don't know whether the disaster did [bring us together more] but it hasn't parted us at all. It hasn't parted anyone. We've still got a wonderful bond here with everyone. I've seen them go through their sorrow... but not a day goes by that any of us forgets this terrible disaster. It lives with you and is as vivid as if it was yesterday.

Even Gerald, who still has mixed feelings about what he sees as his bad luck in the village, feels positive about how the community has come through.

But the community pull together now. You don't hear much talk of it. Yes, the community's back together now and it seems a happier village.

Everyone has moved on to a greater or lesser extent. Though some moved physically away in order to do so, those like Marilyn who chose to stay have no regrets.

My husband found a piece of land about a mile away and built a house. So I don't actually live in the village now. I get all my gossip when I go to see my friend Mary Morse, and obviously the Wives have helped. But I think having children as well helps you because you've got to concentrate on them now, haven't you? And you do get on with your life. I am very happy now. Of course I think of Janette all the time, but I'm happy.

It's funny when you look back and you think, how did I do that? How did I get through it? I think to myself sometimes, how did you manage that?

Then, tired but laughing, Marilyn says: 'I want to stop now!' and her interview comes to a close.

This perhaps is the lasting impression from the testimony of our survivors. Despite the horror of the disaster and the sorrow and anger left in its wake, the people most directly affected – the people of Aberfan – have come through. As former Methodist lay preacher June Vaughan believes, not only have they survived but in so many ways together they have made better lives for themselves and for others.

> There *is* hope. There is the realisation that good can come out of....bad. You know, whatever the opposite of good is. Good can come out of it. It can help to build individuals, help to build groups, help to build churches. In that way we are lucky.

*

To anyone over 60 who still remembers the impact of those terrible black and white news images of October 21st 1966, much less to those who were witness to and victims of the disaster, it seems barely credible that half a century has passed. Is 50 years long enough for old wounds to heal?

This is the wrong question to ask. Time and trauma don't sit easily together: grief, guilt, anger, physical and mental pain can last lifetimes – sometimes even pass between generations. But the passage of time also softens some memories, hardens others. Strong feelings can pass, long-held attitudes and antipathies change. Nothing stands still. No-one 'gets over' a disaster of the suddenness, scale and severity of Aberfan. There are only different ways of surviving.

Lightning Source UK Ltd.
Milton Keynes UK
UKOW02f1956191016

285692UK00001B/1/P